BASEBALL CARDS

Text by
Larry Schwartz

PRICE STERN SLOAN
Los Angeles

Officially licensed by Major League Baseball

Official Licensee

© 1988 MLBPA
© MSA

An MBKA Production

Printed and bound in Hong Kong.

TEAM LEADERS

Hall of Famers
Earl Averill
Ed Barrow (Executive)
Ty Cobb
Mickey Cochrane
Sam Crawford
Billy Evans (Executive)
Rick Ferrell (Executive)
Charlie Gehringer
Goose Goslin
Hank Greenberg
Bucky Harris (Manager)
Harry Heilmann
Waite Hoyt
Hughie Jennings (Manager)
Al Kaline
George Kell
Heinie Manush
Eddie Mathews
Al Simmons
Sam Thompson

Twenty Game Winners
1901 - Roscoe Miller (23)
1905 - Ed Killian (23)
      George Mullin (21)
1906 - George Mullin (21)
1907 - Bill Donovan (25)
      Ed Killian (25)
      George Mullin (20)
1908 - Ed Summers (24)
1909 - George Mullin (29)
      Ed Willett (22)
1910 - George Mullin (21)
1914 - Harry Coveleski (22)
1915 - George Dauss (24)
      Harry Coveleski (22)
1916 - Harry Coveleski (21)
1919 - George Dauss (21)
1923 - George Dauss (21)
1934 - Schoolboy Rowe (24)
      Tommy Bridges (22)
1935 - Tommy Bridges (21)
1936 - Tommy Bridges (23)
*1939 - Bobo Newsom (20)

1940 - Bobo Newsom (21)
1943 - Dizzy Trout (20)
1944 - Hal Newhouser (29)
      Dizzy Trout (27)
1945 - Hal Newhouser (25)
1946 - Hal Newhouser (26)
1948 - Hal Newhouser (21)
1956 - Frank Lary (21)
      Billy Hoeft (20)
1957 - Jim Bunning (20)
1961 - Frank Lary (23)
1966 - Denny McLain (20)
1967 - Earl Wilson (22)
1968 - Denny McLain (31)
1969 - Denny McLain (24)
1971 - Mickey Lolich (25)
1972 - Mickey Lolich (22)
1973 - Joe Coleman (23)
1983 - Jack Morris (20)
1986 - Jack Morris (21)
*Pitched with Browns (3) and
Tigers (17).

No-Hitters
7-04-12 George Mullin (vs. Browns)
5-15-52 Virgil Trucks (vs. Senators)
8-25-52 Virgil Trucks (at New York)
7-20-58 Jim Bunning (at Boston)
4-07-84 Jack Morris (at Chicago)

League Leaders

Home Runs
1908 - Sam Crawford (7)
1909 - Ty Cobb (9)
*1935 - Hank Greenberg (36)
1938 - Hank Greenberg (58)
1940 - Hank Greenberg (41)
1943 - Rudy York (34)
1946 - Hank Greenberg (44)
1985 - Darrell Evans (40)
*Tied

Runs Batted In
1907 - Ty Cobb (116)
1908 - Ty Cobb (101)
1909 - Ty Cobb (115)
1910 - Sam Crawford (115)
1911 - Ty Cobb (144)
1914 - Sam Crawford (112)
1915 - Sam Crawford (116)
1917 - Bobby Veach (115)
*1918 - Bobby Veach (74)
1935 - Hank Greenberg (170)
1937 - Hank Greenberg (183)
1940 - Hank Greenberg (150)
1943 - Rudy York (118)
1946 - Hank Greenberg (127)
*1955 - Ray Boone (116)
*Tied

League Leaders

Batting Average
1907 - Ty Cobb (.350)
1908 - Ty Cobb (.324)
1909 - Ty Cobb (.377)
1910 - Ty Cobb (.385)
1911 - Ty Cobb (.420)
1912 - Ty Cobb (.410)
1913 - Ty Cobb (.390)
1914 - Ty Cobb (.368)
1915 - Ty Cobb (.369)
1917 - Ty Cobb (.383)
1918 - Ty Cobb (.382)
1919 - Ty Cobb (.384)
1921 - Harry Heilmann (.394)
1923 - Harry Heilmann (.403)
1925 - Harry Heilmann (.393)
1926 - Heinie Manush (.378)
1927 - Harry Heilmann (.398)
*1932 - Dale Alexander (.367)
1937 - Charlie Gehringer (.371)
1949 - George Kell (.343)
1955 - Al Kaline (.340)
1959 - Harvey Kuenn (.353)
1961 - Norm Cash (.361)
* Played with Tigers and Red Sox

Wins
1909 - George Mullin (29)
1936 - Tommy Bridges (23)
*1943 - Dizzy Trout (20)
1944 - Hal Newhouser (29)
1945 - Hal Newhouser (25)
*1946 - Hal Newhouser (26)
1948 - Hal Newhouser (21)
1956 - Frank Lary (21)
*1957 - Jim Bunning (20)
*1967 - Earl Wilson (22)
1968 - Denny McLain (31)
1969 - Denny McLain (24)
1971 - Mickey Lolich (25)
*1981 - Jack Morris (14)
*Tied

Strikeouts
1935 - Tommy Bridges (163)
1936 - Tommy Bridges (175)
1944 - Hal Newhouser (187)
1945 - Hal Newhouser (212)
1949 - Virgil Trucks (153)
1959 - Jim Bunning (201)
1960 - Jim Bunning (201)
1971 - Mickey Lolich (308)
1983 - Jack Morris (232)

Earned Run Average
1944 - Dizzy Trout (2.12)
1945 - Hal Newhouser (1.81)
1946 - Hal Newhouser (1.94)
*1951 - Saul Rogovin (2.78)
1962 - Hank Aguirre (2.21)
1976 - Mark Fidrych (2.34)
*Pitched with Tigers and White Sox.

Most Valuable Players
1911 - Ty Cobb
1934 - Mickey Cochrane
1935 - Hank Greenberg
1937 - Charlie Gehringer
1940 - Hank Greenberg
1944 - Hal Newhouser
1945 - Hal Newhouser
1968 - Denny McLain
1984 - Willie Hernandez

Rookies of the Year
1953 - Harvey Kuenn
1976 - Mark Fidrych
1978 - Lou Whitaker

Cy Young Award Winners
1968 - Denny McLain
*1969 - Denny McLain
1984 - Willie Hernandez
*Tied

World Series Appearances
1907	1934	*1945
1908	*1935	*1968
1909	1940	*1984

*World Champions

Club Records

Batting
Runs . . . . Ty Cobb (147, 1911)
Hits . . . . Ty Cobb (248, 1911)
Doubles . . . . Hank Greenberg (63, 1934)
Triples . . . . Sam Crawford (26, 1914)
Home Runs . . . . Hank Greenberg (58, 1938)
Runs Batted In . . . . Hank Greenberg (183, 1937)
Stolen Bases . . . . Ty Cobb (96, 1915)
Batting Average . . . . Ty Cobb (.420, 1911)

Pitching
Games . . . . Willie Hernandez (80, 1984)
Innings . . . . George Mullin (381, 1904)
Wins . . . . Denny McLain (31, 1968)
Strikeouts . . . . Mickey Lolich (308, 1971)
Saves . . . . John Hiller (38, 1973)
Earned Run Average. . . . . . . Hal Newhouser (1.81, 1945)

Compiled by Bill Haber.

1952

The Tigers lost their first eight games and things never improved. For the first time since the American League was formed at the start of the century, the Tigers came in last, 45 games behind the Yankees. Their 50-104 record (45 fewer wins than they achieved two years earlier) was the worst in their history. Red Rolfe was fired as manager on July 5 with the team at 23-49 and pitcher Fred Hutchinson, who first joined the team in 1939, succeeded him. Hutchinson soon gave up pitching though he came back to appear in three games in 1953. While Virgil Trucks went 5-19, two of his victories were no-hitters, making him only the third pitcher to get two in a season. These were the first Tiger no-hitters since George Mullin pitched one in 1912. Art Houtteman (8-20) was one out away from a no-hitter when Cleveland's Harry Simpson broke it up. First baseman Walt Dropo, obtained from Boston in June, tied a major league record with 12 consecutive hits on July 14 and July 15 before being retired in the second game of a doubleheader.

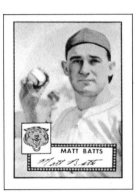

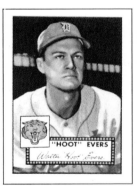

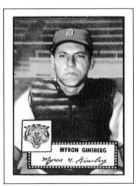

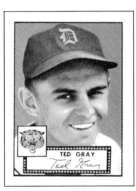

MATT BATTS

"HOOT" EVERS

MYRON GINSBERG

TED GRAY

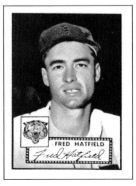

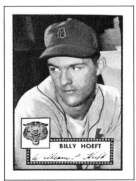

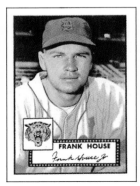

JOHNNY GROTH

FRED HATFIELD

BILLY HOEFT

FRANK HOUSE

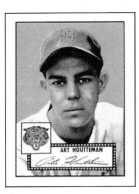

ART HOUTTEMAN

FRED HUTCHINSON

GEORGE KELL

DON KOLLOWAY

JOHNNY LIPON

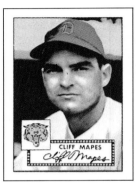

CLIFF MAPES

PAT MULLIN

JERRY PRIDDY

"RED" ROLFE

STEVE SOUCHOCK

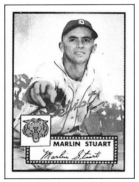

MARLIN STUART

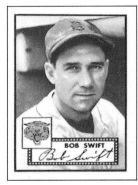

BOB SWIFT

"DIZZY" TROUT

VIRGIL TRUCKS

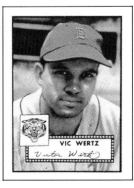

VIC WERTZ

1953

It looked like another last-place finish as the Tigers went 10-31 in the first two months and were 27-60 in the middle of July. But from then on the Tigers went 33-34 to move into sixth place at 60-94, 40½ games behind the Yankees. Hitting was the key to the improvement as Detroit was third in the American League in batting at .266. Shortstop Harvey Kuenn, who received a $55,000 bonus after graduating from Wisconsin in 1952, led the majors in hits with 209 and batted .308, sixth highest in the A.L. He was voted Rookie of the Year. Third baseman Ray Boone, obtained from Cleveland in June in an eight-player trade, finished the season with 26 homers, 114 RBIs (third in the league), 94 runs and a .296 average. He hit four grand slams, two each with the Tigers and Indians.

JIM DELSING
outfielder DETROIT TIGERS

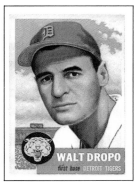
WALT DROPO
first base DETROIT TIGERS

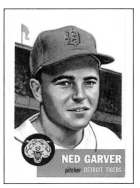
NED GARVER
pitcher DETROIT TIGERS

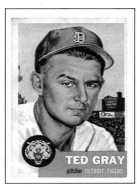
TED GRAY
pitcher DETROIT TIGERS

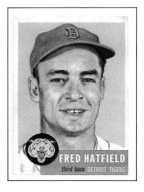
FRED HATFIELD
third base DETROIT TIGERS

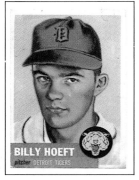
BILLY HOEFT
pitcher DETROIT TIGERS

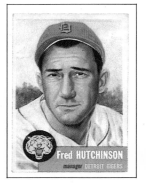
Fred HUTCHINSON
manager DETROIT TIGERS

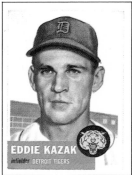
EDDIE KAZAK
infielder DETROIT TIGERS

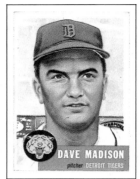

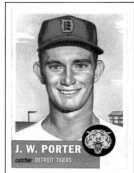

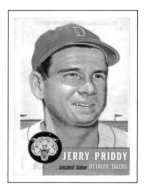

1954

The Tigers just missed finishing in the first division, coming in a game behind fourth-place Boston. However, with their 68-86 record, they were a long way from the top, 43 games behind the Indians. Harvey Kuenn tied for the most hits in the league with Nellie Fox at 201 and his .306 average was sixth. On July 19 he was down at .252 but hit .375 the rest of the year. Nineteen-year-old rookie rightfielder Al Kaline, a future Hall of Famer, did not have an auspicious debut season (.276, 4 homers, 43 RBIs). Pitcher Steve Gromek started 7-1 and finished 18-16 with a 2.74 ERA, fifth best in the league. The Tigers' only other double-figures winner was Ned Garver (14-11, 2.81 ERA). After the season Tiger management rejected manager Fred Hutchinson's demand for a two-year contract, leading to Hutchinson's resignation. Bucky Harris, let go as the Washington Senators' manager, replaced him.

AL ABER
pitcher DETROIT TIGERS

MATT BATTS
catcher DETROIT TIGERS

RENO BERTOIA
infield DETROIT TIGERS

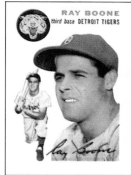

RAY BOONE
third base DETROIT TIGERS

JIM DELSING
outfield Detroit Tigers

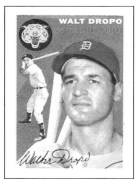

WALT DROPO
Detroit Tigers

NED GARVER
pitcher DETROIT TIGERS

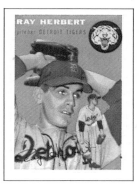

RAY HERBERT
pitcher DETROIT TIGERS

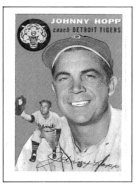

JOHNNY HOPP
coach DETROIT TIGERS

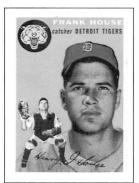

FRANK HOUSE
catcher DETROIT TIGERS

AL KALINE
outfield DETROIT TIGERS

CHARLIE KRESS
first base DETROIT TIGERS

HARVEY KUENN
shortstop DETROIT TIGERS

DON LUND
outfield DETROIT TIGERS

BOB MILLER
pitcher DETROIT TIGERS

JOHNNY PESKY
second base DETROIT TIGERS

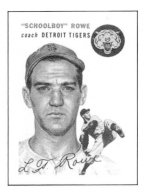

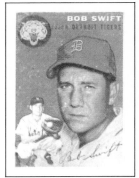

1955

Al Kaline, 20, began showing his greatness. The rightfielder became the youngest player ever to win a batting title when he hit .340. (Kaline was a day younger than another 20-year-old champion, a guy by the name of Cobb.) Kaline also was the only 200-hit man in the majors and had 27 homers, 102 RBIs and scored 121 runs. Ray Boone became the last Tiger to win an RBI title, tying with Jackie Jensen at 116, and Harvey Kuenn batted .306 again (fifth in the league). This hitting kept the Tigers in contention until early August when, though they were in fifth place, they were only 5 ½ games out of first. However, they went 24-28 in the last two months to finish fifth at 79-75 under new manager Bucky Harris, 17 games behind the Yankees. The Tigers played spoiler in the pennant race, sweeping the contending Indians in a three-game series in mid-September.

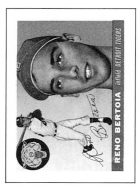

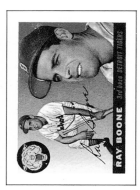

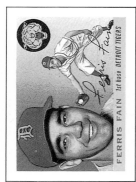

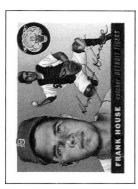
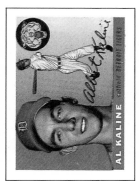
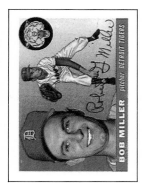

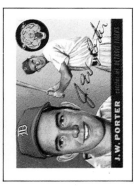

1956

The Tigers were first in the majors with a .279 average and had four .300 hitters. Harvey Kuenn led the A. L. in hits and batted .332; leftfielder Charlie Maxwell had his only .300 season at .326 and also had 28 homers and 87 RBIs; Al Kaline hit .314 with 27 homers and a career-high 128 RBIs; and Ray Boone batted .308 with 25 homers. The Tigers also had two 20-game winners in second-year pitcher Frank Lary, the league's biggest winner with his 21-13 record, and Billy Hoeft (20-14). Still, it wasn't enough to make contenders out of the Tigers as they finished fifth again at 82-72, 15 games behind the Yankees. The Tigers, who were blasted by team president Spike Briggs during a 10-game losing streak in June, had the best record (37-17) of any team in baseball the final two months of the season. Despite this improvement, Bucky Harris quit as manager after the season with coach Jack Tighe replacing him. An 11-man syndicate headed by Detroit native Fred Knorr paid $5.5 million for the team and Briggs Stadium.

AL ABER
pitcher DETROIT TIGERS

"BABE" BIRRER
pitcher DETROIT TIGERS

RAY BOONE
third base DETROIT TIGERS

JIM BRADY
pitcher DETROIT TIGERS

JIM DELSING
outfield DETROIT TIGERS

NED GARVER
pitcher DETROIT TIGERS

STEVE GROMEK
pitcher DETROIT TIGERS

FRED HATFIELD
second base DETROIT TIGERS

BILLY HOEFT
pitcher DETROIT TIGERS

FRANK HOUSE
catcher DETROIT TIGERS

AL KALINE
outfield DETROIT TIGERS

HARVEY KUENN
shortstop DETROIT TIGERS

FRANK LARY
pitcher DETROIT TIGERS

"DUKE" MAAS
pitcher DETROIT TIGERS

BOB MILLER
pitcher DETROIT TIGERS

JIM SMALL
outfiele DETROIT TIGERS

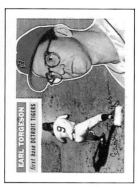

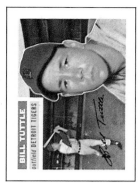

≣1957≣

After six straight second-division finishes, the Tigers broke into the upper half of the league by coming in fourth.Under rookie manager Jack Tighe the Tigers went 78-76, 20 games behind the Yankees. Jim Bunning, who had pitched some for the team the past two years, became the ace of the staff. The righthander (20-8) tied Billy Pierce for most wins in the league and was third with a 2.70 ERA. Frank Lary had a disappointing season (11-16, 3.97 ERA), as did Billy Hoeft (9-11, 3.48 ERA). Eight of Hoeft's wins came after the All-Star Game. Al Kaline also had a strong finish, hitting 17 of his 23 home runs in the last 54 games. Harvey Kuenn, besides slumping to .277 (the first time in his six seasons he hit less than .306), led A.L. shortstops in errors (27). His second baseman partner, Frank Bolling, also led his position in errors (16).

AL **Aber**
DETROIT TIGERS PITCHER

FRANK **Bolling**
DETROIT TIGERS 2ND BASE

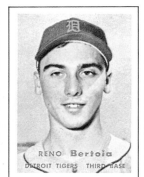

RENO **Bertoia**
DETROIT TIGERS THIRD BASE

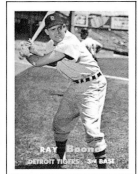

RAY **Boone**
DETROIT TIGERS 3RD BASE

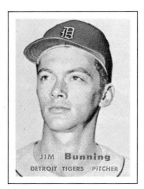

JIM **Bunning**
DETROIT TIGERS PITCHER

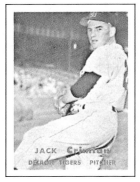

JACK **Crimian**
DETROIT TIGERS PITCHER

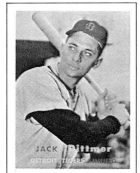

JACK **Dittmer**
DETROIT TIGERS INFIELD

JIM **Finigan**
DETROIT TIGERS 2ND & 3RD BASE

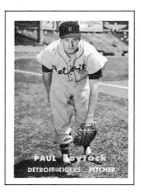

PAUL **Foytack**
DETROIT TIGERS PITCHER

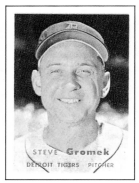

STEVE **Gromek**
DETROIT TIGERS PITCHER

BILLY **Hoeft**
DETROIT TIGERS PITCHER

FRANK **House**
DETROIT TIGERS CATCHER

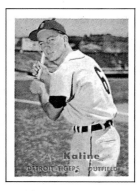

AL **Kaline**
DETROIT TIGERS OUTFIELD

BOB **Kennedy**
DETROIT TIGERS 3RD B.—O.F.

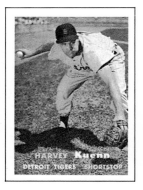

HARVEY **Kuenn**
DETROIT TIGERS SHORTSTOP

FRANK
PITCHER

DON Lee
DETROIT TIGERS PITCHER

DUKE Maas
DETROIT TIGERS PITCHER

CHARLEY Maxwell
DETROIT TIGERS OUTFIELD

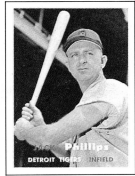

JACK Phillips
DETROIT TIGERS INFIELD

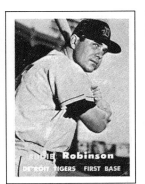

EDDIE Robinson
DETROIT TIGERS FIRST BASE

JIM Small
DETROIT TIGERS OUTFIELD

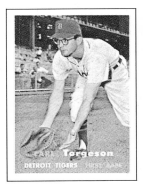

EARL Torgeson
DETROIT TIGERS FIRST BASE

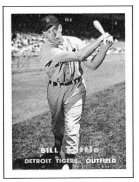

BILL Tuttle
DETROIT TIGERS OUTFIELD

BOB Wilson
DETROIT TIGERS CATCHER

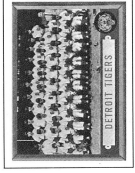

DETROIT TIGERS

1958

Harvey Kuenn, moved from shortstop to centerfield, regained his .300 ways, batting .319, third highest in the league. Al Kaline was next in the batting race at .313. The hitting of the K Kids, though, couldn't save manager Jack Tighe's job. Tighe was fired on June 10 with the Tigers in last place (21-28). Bill Norman, who had been managing Charlestown, took over and the Tigers won nine of 11, including seven straight over the Yankees. But the Tigers played .500 ball the rest of the season to finish at .500 (77-77), fading from second to fifth, 15 games behind New York. Frank Lary was the team's big winner at 16-15, including a 7-1 record against the Yankees, and Paul Foytack was next at 15-13. Jim Bunning was 14-12, with one of the wins being a 3-0 no-hitter of Boston in which he openly talked of getting the feat in the dugout between innings. The last out was made by Ted Williams, who led the league with a .328 average that year.

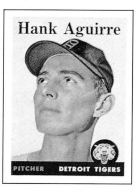

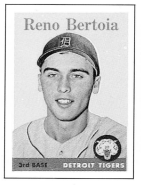

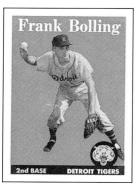

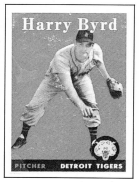

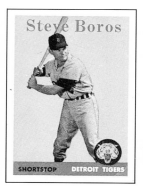

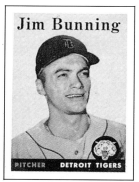

Johnny Groth
OUTFIELD · DETROIT TIGERS

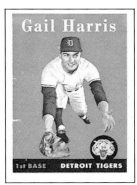

Gail Harris
1st BASE · DETROIT TIGERS

Jim Hegan
CATCHER · DETROIT TIGERS

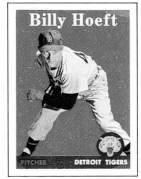

Billy Hoeft
PITCHER · DETROIT TIGERS

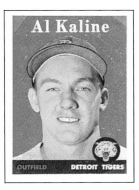

Al Kaline
OUTFIELD · DETROIT TIGERS

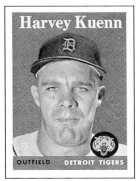

Harvey Kuenn
OUTFIELD · DETROIT TIGERS

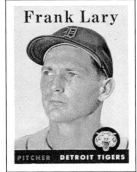

Frank Lary
PITCHER · DETROIT TIGERS

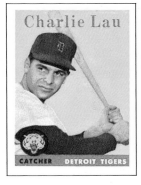

Charlie Lau
CATCHER · DETROIT TIGERS

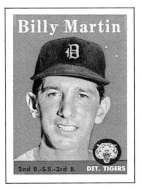

Billy Martin
2nd B.-S.S.-3rd B. · DET. TIGERS

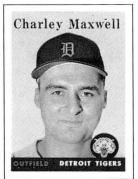

Charley Maxwell
OUTFIELD · DETROIT TIGERS

Tom Morgan
PITCHER · DETROIT TIGERS

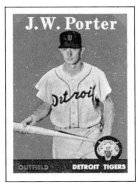

J.W. Porter
OUTFIELD · DETROIT TIGERS

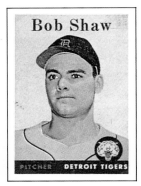

Bob Shaw
PITCHER · DETROIT TIGERS

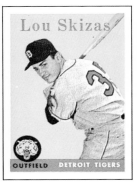

Lou Skizas
OUTFIELD · DETROIT TIGERS

Lou Sleater
PITCHER · DETROIT TIGERS

Bill Taylor
OUTFIELD · DETROIT TIGERS

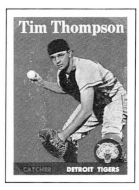

Tim Thompson
CATCHER DETROIT TIGERS

Vito Valentinetti
PITCHER DETROIT TIGERS

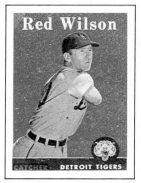

Red Wilson
CATCHER DETROIT TIGERS

Gus Zernial
OUTFIELD DETROIT TIGERS

TIGERS' BIG BATS
HARVEY KUENN • AL KALINE

1959

The K Kids were even better this year. Harvey Kuenn won his only batting championship at .353 and led the A.L. in hits (198) for the fourth time. Al Kaline was next in batting at .327 and, despite suffering a fractured jaw which limited him to 136 games, hit 27 homers (for the third time in five years) and had 94 RBIs. And again their exploits weren't enough to keep another manager from being fired. When the Tigers started 2-15, Bill Norman was gone. Jimmy Dykes, who had been coaching the Pirates, took over and his first move was to insert Charlie Maxwell, who had been hitting .136, back into the lineup. Maxwell responded by hitting four consecutive home runs in a doubleheader sweep of the Yankees. That started the Tigers on a 32-14 streak which moved them to within a half game of first. But then, as in 1958, the team faded. It finished fourth at 76-78, 18 games behind the White Sox. Frank Lary, Jim Bunning and Don Mossi, with 17 wins each, accounted for 65% of the team's wins. Third baseman Eddie Yost, obtained from Washington, led the A.L. in runs (115) and walks (135) and surprisingly hit 21 homers, a career high.

hank aguirre

DETROIT TIGERS
PITCHER

ossie alvarez

DETROIT TIGERS
INFIELD

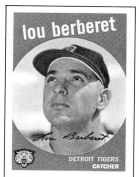

lou berberet

DETROIT TIGERS
CATCHER

frank bolling

DETROIT TIGERS
SECOND BASE

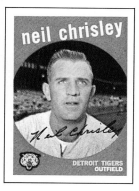

steve boros

DETROIT TIGERS
INFIELD

rocky bridges

DETROIT TIGERS
SHORTSTOP

jim bunning

DETROIT TIGERS
PITCHER

pete burnside

DETROIT TIGERS
PITCHER

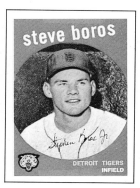

neil chrisley

DETROIT TIGERS
OUTFIELD

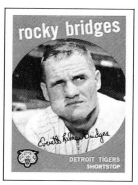

jerry davie

DETROIT TIGERS
PITCHER

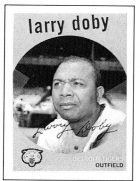

larry doby

DETROIT TIGERS
OUTFIELD

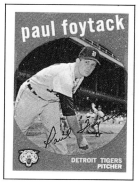

paul foytack

DETROIT TIGERS
PITCHER

tito francona

DETROIT TIGERS
OUTFIELD

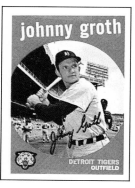

johnny groth

DETROIT TIGERS
OUTFIELD

gail harris

DETROIT TIGERS
FIRST BASE

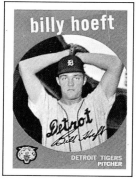

billy hoeft

DETROIT TIGERS
PITCHER

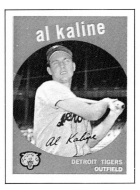

al kaline

DETROIT TIGERS
OUTFIELD

The Sporting News

AL KALINE
RIGHT FIELD   AMERICAN LEAGUE
'59 ALL STAR SELECTION

harvey kuenn

DETROIT TIGERS
OUTFIELD

frank lary

DETROIT TIGERS
PITCHER

The Sporting News
ROOKIE STARS OF 1959

DON LEE
TIGERS PITCHER

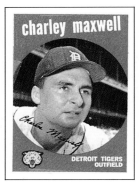

charley maxwell

DETROIT TIGERS
OUTFIELD

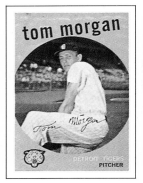

tom morgan

DETROIT TIGERS
PITCHER

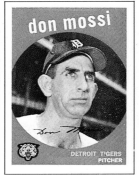

don mossi

DETROIT TIGERS
PITCHER

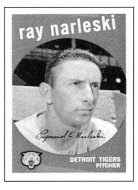

ray narleski

DETROIT TIGERS
PITCHER

larry osborne

DETROIT TIGERS
FIRST BASE

george susce

DETROIT TIGERS
PITCHER

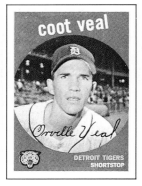

coot veal

DETROIT TIGERS
SHORTSTOP

ozzie virgil

DETROIT TIGERS
THIRD BASE

herm wehmeier

DETROIT TIGERS
PITCHER

red wilson

DETROIT TIGERS
CATCHER

eddie yost

DETROIT TIGERS
THIRD BASE

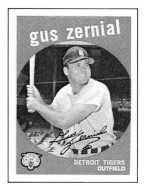

1960

The Tigers made two interesting trades with the Indians. On April 17, the Tigers dealt Harvey Kuenn, a .300 hitter in seven of his eight seasons, to Cleveland for home run champion Rocky Colavito. The rightfielder led the team with 35 homers and 87 RBIs. However, that deal was just a warmup for perhaps the strangest trade ever. Detroit was in sixth place at 44-52 when manager Jimmy Dykes was sent to Cleveland for Indians' manager Joe Gordon. The trade didn't help either team. The Tigers went 26-31 under Gordon and remained in sixth. After finishing 71-83, 26 games behind the Yankees, Gordon quit, citing interference by team president Bill DeWitt. A week later, Gordon became manager of his third team that season, Kansas City. John Fetzer, a minority owner, gained controlling interest in the team by buying another 20% in October.

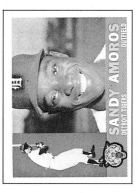

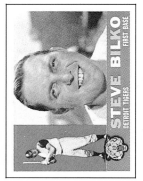

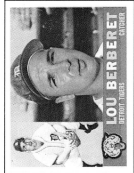

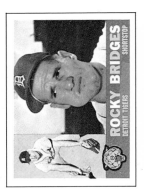
FRANK BOLLING SECOND BASE
DETROIT TIGERS

ROCKY BRIDGES SHORTSTOP
DETROIT TIGERS

SPORT MAGAZINE
1960
ROOKIE
STAR
BOB BRUCE DETROIT TIGERS · PITCHER

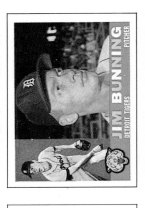
JIM BUNNING PITCHER
DETROIT TIGERS

PETE BURNSIDE PITCHER
DETROIT TIGERS

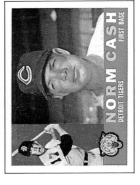
NORM CASH FIRST BASE
DETROIT TIGERS

NEIL CHRISLEY OUTFIELD
DETROIT TIGERS

JERRY DAVIE PITCHER
DETROIT TIGERS

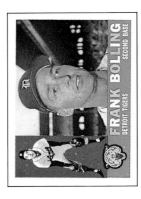
TIGERS
JIMMIE DYKES
MANAGER · DETROIT

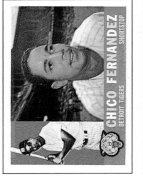
CHICO FERNANDEZ SHORTSTOP
DETROIT TIGERS

PAUL FOYTACK PITCHER
DETROIT TIGERS

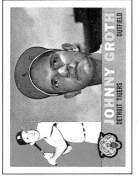
JOHNNY GROTH OUTFIELD
DETROIT TIGERS

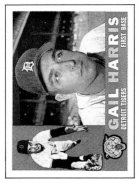
GAIL HARRIS FIRST BASE
DETROIT TIGERS

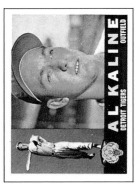
AL KALINE OUTFIELD
DETROIT TIGERS

SPORT MAGAZINE '60 ALL-STAR SELECTION
AL KALINE Outfield/American League

HARVEY KUENN OUTFIELD
DETROIT TIGERS

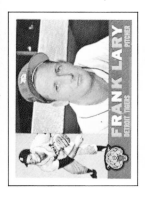

FRANK LARY
PITCHER
DETROIT TIGERS

CHARLIE MAXWELL
OUTFIELD
DETROIT TIGERS

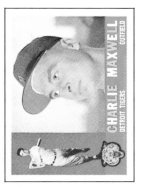

TOM MORGAN
PITCHER
DETROIT TIGERS

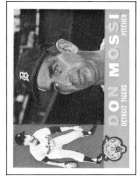

DON MOSSI
PITCHER
DETROIT TIGERS

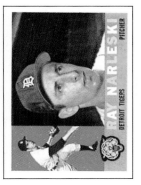

RAY NARLESKI
PITCHER
DETROIT TIGERS

LARRY OSBORNE
FIRST BASE
DETROIT TIGERS

SPORT MAGAZINE
1960
ROOKIE STAR
JIM PROCTOR
DETROIT TIGERS · PITCHER

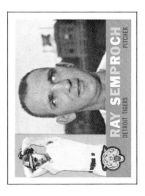

RAY SEMPROCH
PITCHER
DETROIT TIGERS

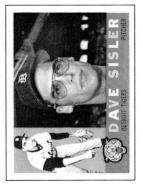

DAVE SISLER
PITCHER
DETROIT TIGERS

RED WILSON
CATCHER
DETROIT TIGERS

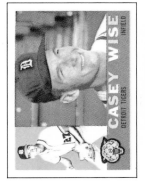

CASEY WISE
INFIELD
DETROIT TIGERS

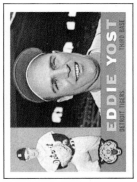

EDDIE YOST
THIRD BASE
DETROIT TIGERS

FERRICK
APPLING
HITCHCOCK
DETROIT TIGERS
COACHES

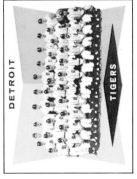

DETROIT
TIGERS

1961

In most seasons, Norm Cash's stats would have been money in the bank to win him the Triple Crown. The first baseman hit .361 with 41 homers and 132 RBIs. Unfortunately for him, this was the year Roger Maris hit his record 61 homers with 142 RBIs. Cash's consolation prize was the batting title. His teammate, Rocky Colavito, also beat him in two categories with 45 homers and 140 RBIs. Al Kaline bounced back from a .278 season to hit .324. On the mound, the Tigers had five double-figure winners, led by Frank Lary (23-9). The team started off fast under new manager Bob Scheffing, going 17-5. They were 1½ games ahead of the Yankees at the All-Star break and were in first in late July. But in a three-game showdown in early September, the Yankees swept before 171,503 fans at Yankee Stadium. The Tigers lost five more in a row and were out of the race. They finished second, eight games behind the Yankees, at 101-61, the first time they won more than 100 games since 1934. Helping their cause was expansion as Los Angeles and Washington joined to make it a 10-team league.

HANK AGUIRRE — Pitcher — Detroit Tigers

STEVE BOROS — Third Base — Detroit Tigers

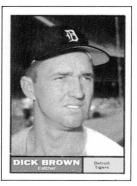

DICK BROWN — Catcher — Detroit Tigers

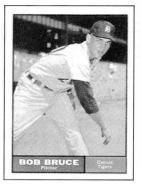

BOB BRUCE — Pitcher — Detroit Tigers

BILL BRUTON — Outfield — Detroit Tigers

JIM BUNNING — Pitcher — Detroit Tigers

NORM CASH — First Base — Detroit Tigers

HARRY CHITI — Catcher — Detroit Tigers

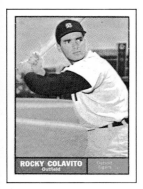

ROCKY COLAVITO
Outfield — Detroit Tigers

CHUCK COTTIER
Second Base-Shortstop — Detroit Tigers

JIM DONOHUE
Pitcher — Detroit Tigers

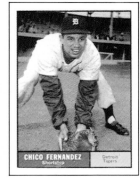

CHICO FERNANDEZ
Shortstop — Detroit Tigers

BILL FISCHER
Pitcher — Detroit Tigers

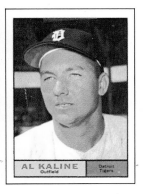

TERRY FOX
Pitcher — Detroit Tigers

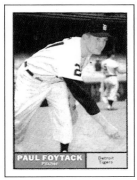

PAUL FOYTACK
Pitcher — Detroit Tigers

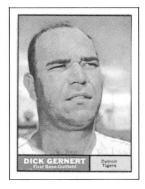

DICK GERNERT
First Base-Outfield — Detroit Tigers

AL KALINE
Outfield — Detroit Tigers

Sporting News — AL KALINE - LF

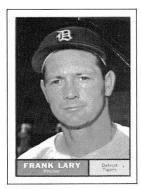

FRANK LARY
Pitcher — Detroit Tigers

CHARLIE MAXWELL
Outfield — Detroit Tigers

DON MOSSI
Pitcher — Detroit Tigers

LARRY OSBORNE
First Baser — Detroit Tigers

PHIL REGAN
Pitcher — Detroit Tigers

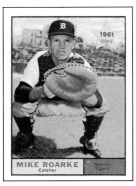

MIKE ROARKE
Catcher — Detroit Tigers

BOB SCHEFFING
Mgr.   Detroit Tigers

GEORGE THOMAS
Outfield   Detroit Tigers

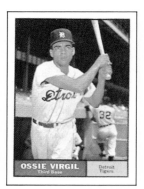

OSSIE VIRGIL
Third Base   Detroit Tigers

JAKE WOOD
Second Base   Detroit Tigers

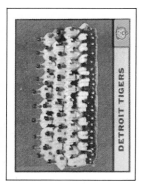

DETROIT TIGERS

1962

The Tigers had plenty of power, setting a team record by hitting 209 home runs. Norm Cash led with 39, Rocky Colavito had 37, Al Kaline (despite playing only 100 games because of injuries) hit a career-high 29, and shortstop Chico Fernandez, whose previous best was six, belted 20. But despite leading the majors in dingers, the Tigers didn't come close to the pennant. They went 85-76 to finish fourth, 10½ games behind the Yankees. And to get that high they had to win 12 of their last 15 games. One Tiger who wasn't much of a hitter was Hank Aguirre, who went 2-for-75 (.027). But he was outstanding on the mound, going 16-8 and leading the majors with a 2.21 ERA. Jim Bunning went 19-10, but Frank Lary, bothered by a sore arm, pitched only 80 innings and went from 23-9 to 2-6. Cash dropped 118 points in batting average, from .361 to .243, the biggest one-season fall for any batting champ.

HANK
AGUIRRE
DET. TIGERS PITCHER

GEORGE
ALUSIK
DETROIT TIGERS OF

STEVE
BOROS
DETROIT TIGERS 3B

DICK
BROWN
DET. TIGERS CATCHER

BILL
BRUTON
DETROIT TIGERS OF

JIM
BUNNING
DETROIT TIGERS P

NORM
CASH
DETROIT TIGERS 1B

The Sporting News
AMERICAN LEAGUE ALL-STAR

NORM
CASH
1 BASE

ROCKY
COLAVITO
DETROIT TIGERS OF

COLAVITO'S POWER

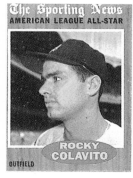

The Sporting News
AMERICAN LEAGUE ALL-STAR

ROCKY
COLAVITO
OUTFIELD

CHICO
FERNANDEZ
DETROIT TIGERS SS

TERRY
FOX
DET. TIGERS PITCHER

PAUL
FOYTACK
DETROIT TIGERS P

SAM
JONES
DETROIT TIGERS P

AL
KALINE
DETROIT TIGERS OF

The Sporting News
AMERICAN LEAGUE ALL-STAR

AL KALINE
OUTFIELD

RON
KLINE
DETROIT TIGERS P

1962 ROOKIE

HOWIE
KOPLITZ
DETROIT TIGERS P

The Sporting News
AMERICAN LEAGUE ALL-STAR

FRANK LARY
R H PITCHER

CHARLEY
MAXWELL
DETROIT TIGERS OF

DICK
McAULIFFE
DET. TIGERS SS-3B

BUBBA
MORTON
DETROIT TIGERS OF

DON
MOSSI
DETROIT TIGERS P

LARRY
OSBORNE
DETROIT TIGERS 1B

PHIL
REGAN
DETROIT TIGERS P

MIKE
ROARKE
DETROIT TIGERS C

BOB
SCHEFFING
DETROIT TIGERS MGR.

1962 ROOKIE

DON
WERT
DET. TIGERS 3B-SS

VIC
WERTZ
DETROIT TIGERS 1B

TOPPS 1961 ALL-STAR ROOKIE

JAKE
WOOD
DETROIT TIGERS 2B

BOB'S PUPILS
DETROIT TIGERS

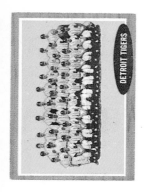

1963

The Tigers started off badly and when they were 24-36, on June 17, Bob Scheffing was fired as manager and replaced by Chuck Dressen, then scouting for the Dodgers. Under Dressen, the team went 55-47, including 22-8 in August, as it moved from ninth into a tie for fifth at 79-83, 25½ games behind the Yankees. Frank Lary spent two months in the minors because of a shoulder ailment and was 4-9 for the Tigers. Phil Regan picked up some of the slack by going 13-3 under Dressen to finish with a career-high 15 wins against 9 losses. Al Kaline was second in the A.L. in batting at .312 and though he would play 11 more seasons this was his last 100-RBI year (at 101). The Tigers did some major housecleaning after the season, sending Rocky Colavito (his 22 homers were his fewest in seven years) to Kansas City and Jim Bunning (12-13) to Philadelphia. Bunning, who won 118 games for the Tigers, would win 106 more in the N.L.

HANK AGUIRRE
DET. TIGERS   PITCHER

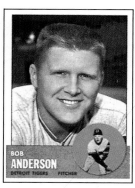

BOB ANDERSON
DETROIT TIGERS   PITCHER

BILL BRUTON
DETROIT TIGERS   OF

JIM BUNNING
DETROIT TIGERS   P

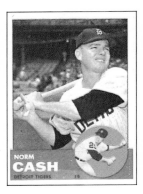

NORM
CASH
DETROIT TIGERS 1B

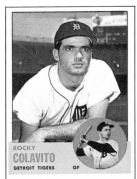

ROCKY
COLAVITO
DETROIT TIGERS OF

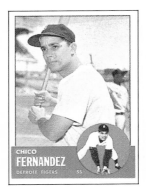

CHICO
FERNANDEZ
DETROIT TIGERS SS

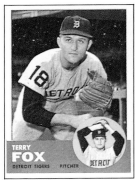

TERRY
FOX
DETROIT TIGERS PITCHER

PAUL
FOYTACK
DETROIT TIGERS P

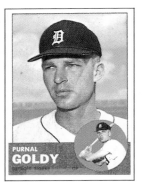

PURNAL
GOLDY
DETROIT TIGERS OF

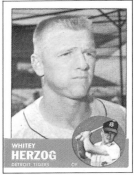

WHITEY
HERZOG
DETROIT TIGERS OF

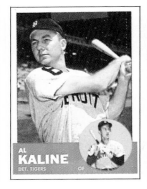

AL
KALINE
DET. TIGERS OF

RON
KLINE
DET. TIGERS PITCHER

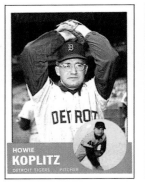

HOWIE
KOPLITZ
DETROIT TIGERS PITCHER

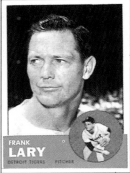

FRANK
LARY
DETROIT TIGERS PITCHER

DICK
McAULIFFE
DET. TIGERS 2B

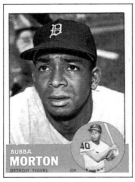

BUBBA
MORTON
DETROIT TIGERS OF

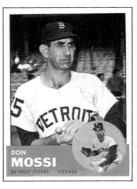

DON
MOSSI
DETROIT TIGERS PITCHER

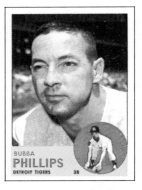

BUBBA
PHILLIPS
DETROIT TIGERS 3B

PHIL
REGAN
DETROIT TIGERS PITCHER

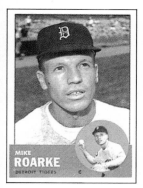

MIKE
ROARKE
DETROIT TIGERS   C

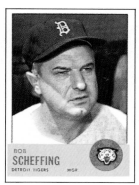

BOB
SCHEFFING
DETROIT TIGERS   MGR

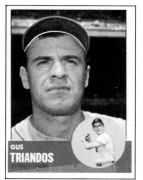

GUS
TRIANDOS

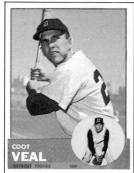

COOT
VEAL
DETROIT TIGERS

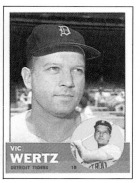

VIC
WERTZ
DETROIT TIGERS   1B

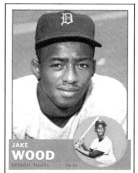

JAKE
WOOD
DETROIT TIGERS   2B-SS

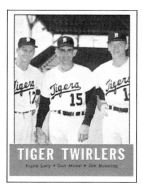

TIGER TWIRLERS
Frank Lary • Don Mossi • Jim Bunning

DETROIT TIGERS

≡1964≡

The Tigers were in eighth, 32-38, at the end of June and were in seventh at the end of July. Then they went 35-22 the rest of the way — the best record in the A.L. — to move up to fourth at 85-77, 14 games behind the Yankees. Home attendance fell to 816,139, the lowest since 1943. Only two pitchers won more than eight games: Dave Wickersham, obtained from Kansas City in the Rocky Colavito trade, had a career-best 19 wins against 12 losses and Mickey Lolich went 18-9 with six shutouts. Bill Freehan, in his second season, hit .300 to become the first Tiger catcher since Mickey Cochrane in 1935 to reach .300. He also had 18 homers and 80 RBIs. Al Kaline, hindered by injuries, batted .293 but with only 17 homers and 68 RBIs. Shortstop Dick McAuliffe was the team leader in home runs with a career-high 24, one more than Norm Cash.

TIGERS

HANK AGUIRRE · pitcher

TIGERS

GATES BROWN · outfield

TIGERS

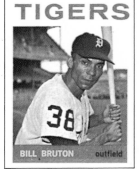
BILL BRUTON · outfield

TIGERS

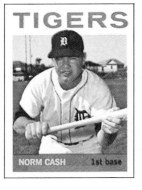
NORM CASH · 1st base

TIGERS

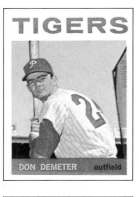
DON DEMETER · outfield

TIGERS

CHUCK DRESSEN · manager

TIGERS

BILL FAUL · pitcher

TIGERS

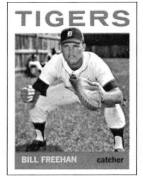
BILL FREEHAN · catcher

TIGERS

TERRY FOX · pitcher

TIGERS

AL KALINE · outfielder

TIGERS

FRANK LARY · pitcher

TIGERS

MICKEY LOLICH · pitcher

TIGERS

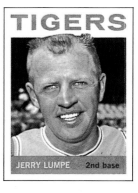
JERRY LUMPE · 2nd base

TIGERS

DICK McAULIFFE · ss

TIGERS

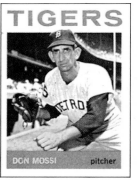
DON MOSSI · pitcher

TIGERS

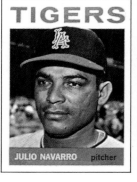
JULIO NAVARRO · pitcher

TIGERS

BUBBA PHILLIPS   3b-of

TIGERS

ED RAKOW   pitcher

TIGERS

PHIL REGAN   pitcher

TIGERS

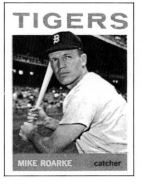

MIKE ROARKE   catcher

TIGERS

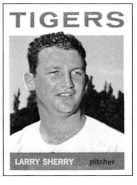

LARRY SHERRY   pitcher

TIGERS

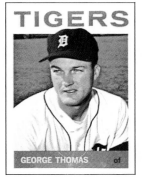

GEORGE THOMAS   of

TIGERS

DON WERT   3rd base

TIGERS

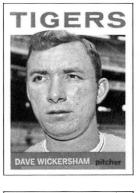

DAVE WICKERSHAM   pitcher

TIGERS

JAKE WOOD   3b-of

1964 ROOKIE STARS
TIGERS

FRITZ FISHER — PITCHER

FRED GLADDING — PITCHER

1964 ROOKIE STARS
TIGERS

WILLIE HORTON — OUTFIELD

JOE SPARMA — PITCHER

DETROIT TIGERS

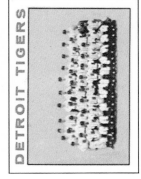

1965

For the past decade, finishing 12 games ahead of the Yanks would mean a pennant. But not this year. The Tigers, who finished a dozen games ahead of New York, came in 13 games behind the Twins in fourth place at 89-73. Chuck Dressen, 66, suffered a heart attack in spring training and coach Bob Swift took over. The team was 24-18, three games out of first, when Dressen returned on Memorial Day. The Tigers still were in second in mid-August before fading. Denny McLain, 21, came on the scene in a big way. After starting 1-3, he won eight straight and finished 16-6 with a 2.62 ERA. He also pitched a one-hitter. Mickey Lolich went 15-9, Hank Aguirre 14-10 and Joe Sparma 13-8, but Dave Wickersham lost eight straight and fell to 9-14. Al Kaline, who played in only 125 games because of injuries, led the Tigers with a .281 average. Norm Cash had 30 homers and leftfielder Willie Horton hit 29 with 104 RBIs.

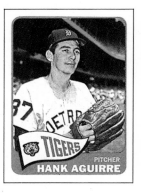
PITCHER
HANK AGUIRRE

OUTFIELD
GATES BROWN

1st BASE
NORM CASH

OUTFIELD
DON DEMETER

MANAGER
CHUCK DRESSEN

PITCHER
TERRY FOX

CATCHER
BILL FREEHAN

PITCHER
FRED GLADDING

JACK HAMILTON · PITCHER

BILLY HOEFT · PITCHER

WILLIE HORTON · OUTFIELD

AL KALINE · OUTFIELD

MICKEY LOLICH · PITCHER

JERRY LUMPE · 2nd BASE

DICK McAULIFFE · SHORTSTOP

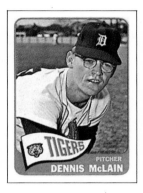

DENNIS McLAIN · PITCHER

JULIO NAVARRO · PITCHER

BUBBA PHILLIPS · OF-3rd BASE

ED RAKOW · PITCHER

PHIL REGAN · PITCHER

LARRY SHERRY · PITCHER

GEORGE SMITH · 2nd BASE

JOE SPARMA · PITCHER

GEORGE THOMAS · OUTFIELD

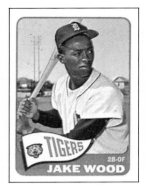

1966

Manager Chuck Dressen suffered his second heart attack in two years and died three months later. Coach Bob Swift, the interim manager, was found to have cancer and died soon after the season. Another coach, Frank Skaff, managed the last 79 games. In October the Tigers signed Mayo Smith, a scout for the Yankees who last managed in 1959, to a two-year contract as manager. On June 24 the Tigers were just 1½ games out of first after going on a 19-5 tear. Five weeks later they were 13½ out. They finished third at 88-74, 10 games behind the Orioles. Pitchers dominated the game and the league batting average was .240; the Tigers' .251 was second best. Al Kaline was third in the league at .288 and Norm Cash was sixth at .279. Kaline tied his career high with 29 homers, three fewer than Cash. Denny McLain went 20-14, including two one-hitters. Earl Wilson, obtained from Boston in June, won nine straight for the Tigers and was 13-6 with them.

HANK AGUIRRE pitcher

GATES BROWN outfield

NORM CASH 1st base

DON DEMETER outfield

CHUCK DRESSEN manager

TERRY FOX pitcher

BILL FREEHAN catcher

FRED GLADDING pitcher

WILLIE HORTON outfield

AL KALINE outfield

MICKEY LOLICH pitcher

JERRY LUMPE 2nd base

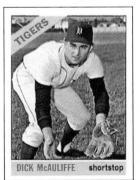

DICK McAULIFFE shortstop

ORLANDO McFARLANE catcher

DENNY McLAIN pitcher

BILL MONBOUQUETTE pitcher

JULIO NAVARRO   pitcher

RON NISCHWITZ   pitcher

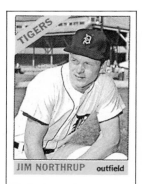

JIM NORTHRUP   outfield

RAY OYLER   shortstop

ORLANDO PENA   pitcher

LARRY SHERRY   pitcher

JOE SPARMA   pitcher

MICKEY STANLEY   outfield

JOHN SULLIVAN   catcher

DICK TRACEWSKI   infield

DON WERT   3b

DAVE WICKERSHAM   ...cher

JAKE WOOD   infield

1966 ROOKIE STARS
TIGERS
JOHN HILLER   pitcher
FRITZ FISHER   pitcher

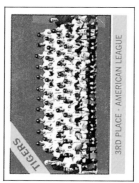

TIGERS   3RD PLACE · AMERICAN LEAGUE

1967

In one of the best pennant races in history, the Tigers entered the last day of the season a half game behind Boston and Minnesota. The Red Sox beat the Twins, but the Tigers, after defeating the Angels in the first game of a doubleheader, lost the second and Boston won the pennant. The Tigers and Twins tied at 91-71, one game out. Earl Wilson (22-11) tied for the most wins in the majors and was Detroit's biggest winner since Hal Newhouser won 26 in 1946. Joe Sparma went 16-9 and Denny McLain 17-16. Mickey Lolich was 8-12 going into September then went 6-1, including three shutouts between Sept. 22 and 30. Bill Freehan led all major league catchers with 74 RBIs, tied for the most homers (20) with Joe Torre and hit .282. Al Kaline was third in the league in batting at .308 and hit 25 homers and knocked in 78 runs (winning Detroit's triple crown) despite missing 26 games after breaking a bone in his right hand while slamming a bat on June 27. Dick McAuliffe, switched from shortstop to second base by new manager Mayo Smith, had 22 homers, but batted only .239.

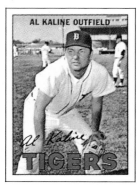

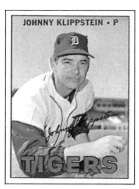

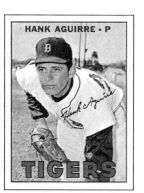

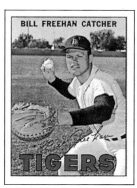

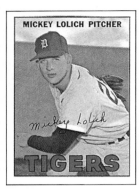

MICKEY LOLICH PITCHER

TIGERS

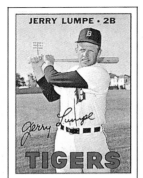

JERRY LUMPE • 2B

TIGERS

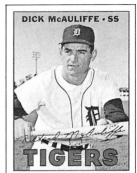

DICK McAULIFFE • SS

TIGERS

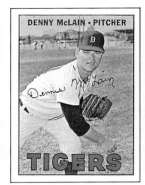

DENNY McLAIN • PITCHER

TIGERS

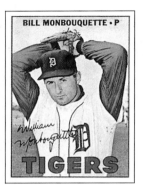

BILL MONBOUQUETTE • P

TIGERS

JIM NORTHRUP • OUTFIELD

TIGERS

RAY OYLER • SHORTSTOP

TIGERS

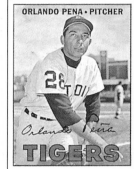

ORLANDO PENA • PITCHER

TIGERS

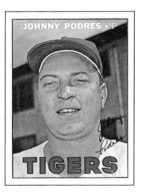

JOHNNY PODRES • P

TIGERS

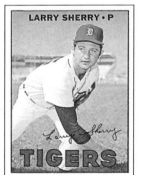

LARRY SHERRY • P

TIGERS

MAYO SMITH • MANAGER

TIGERS

JOE SPARMA PITCHER

TIGERS

MICKEY STANLEY • OF

TIGERS

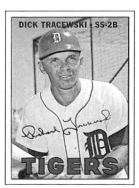

DICK TRACEWSKI • SS-2B

TIGERS

DON WERT • 3B

TIGERS

DAVE WICKERSHAM • P

TIGERS

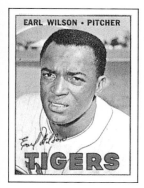

1968

It was the Year of the Tigers. Detroit romped to its first pennant since 1945 by going 103-59, finishing 12 games ahead of Baltimore. From the seventh inning on, the Tigers won 40 times. And they showed their comeback character again in the World Series, coming from three games to one behind the Cards to win the last three games. Mickey Lolich, who was 10-2 the last two months of the regular season to finish 17-9, was the MVP of the World Series with three victories, including outpitching Bob Gibson in the seventh game. Manager Mayo Smith made a gutsy move in the Series, shifting Mickey Stanley (no errors in centerfield all season) to shortstop (removing .135 batter Ray Oyler) to get outfielders Al Kaline, Jim Northrup and Willie Horton all into the lineup. In the regular season, it was Denny McLain who dominated. He was the first 31-game winner since Lefty Grove in 1931. In going 31-6, he pitched 28 complete games, struck out 280 in 336 innings and had a 1.96 ERA. He was the first pitcher ever to be unanimously elected MVP. Of course, he also won the Cy Young Award unanimously. Bill Freehan had career highs in homers (25) and RBIs (84) and was second in MVP balloting. Willie Horton was fourth (.285, 36 homers, 85 RBIs). Dick McAuliffe led the A.L. in runs scored (95), the lowest winning total since 1918.

GATES
BROWN

OUTFIELD
TIGERS

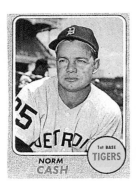

NORM
CASH

1st BASE
TIGERS

PAT
DOBSON

PITCHER
TIGERS

The Sporting News
ALL STAR
SELECTION
68

BILL FREEHAN
CATCHER   AMERICAN LEAGUE

BILL
FREEHAN

CATCHER
TIGERS

JOHN
HILLER

PITCHER
TIGERS

WILLIE
HORTON

OUTFIELD
TIGERS

AL
KALINE

OUTFIELD
TIGERS

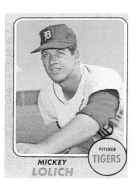

MICKEY
LOLICH

PITCHER
TIGERS

MIKE
MARSHALL

PITCHER
TIGERS

ED
MATHEWS

3B-1B
TIGERS

DICK
McAULIFFE

2nd BASE
TIGERS

DENNY
McLAIN

PITCHER
TIGERS

JIM
NORTHRUP

OUTFIELD
TIGERS

RAY
OYLER

SS
TIGERS

JIMMIE
PRICE

CATCHER
TIGERS

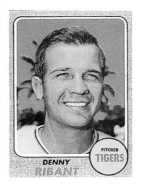

DENNY
RIBANT
PITCHER TIGERS

MAYO
SMITH
MANAGER TIGERS

JOE
SPARMA
PITCHER TIGERS

MICKEY
STANLEY
OUTFIELD TIGERS

DICK
TRACEWSKI
SS-2B TIGERS

DON
WERT
3rd BASE TIGERS

EARL
WILSON
PITCHER TIGERS

1968 ROOKIE STARS

DARYL PATTERSON • P

TOM MATCHICK • SS

TIGERS

1968 ROOKIE STARS

FRED LASHER • P

GEORGE KORINCE • P

TIGERS

TIGERS

AMERICAN LEAGUE

1969

Thud. That noise was the Tigers coming back to earth. Though they had a 90-72 record, they finished second in the A.L. East, 19 games behind Baltimore. (The addition of expansion teams in Seattle and Kansas City led to the league switching to two six-team divisions.) Denny McLain again was outstanding (24-9, 2.80 ERA), leading the league in wins and the majors in shutouts (nine). He tied with Mike Cuellar (23-11, 2.38 ERA) for the Cy Young Award. Mickey Lolich was 19-11, losing 2-1 on the last day to deprive him of a 20-game season. Jim Northrup, whose triple was the game-winning hit in the seventh game of the 1968 Series, led the Tigers at .295, aided by a six-for-six day against Oakland. Willie Horton, who left the team for four days when booed and was fined $1,360, led the Tigers with 91 RBIs, 12 coming on three grand slams.

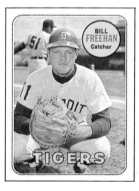

The Sporting News
AMERICAN LEAGUE·ALL-STARS

WILLIE HORTON
Outfield
TIGERS

The Sporting News
1968 WORLD SERIES SPECIAL
KALINE'S KEY HIT
SPARKS TIGER RALLY
Sends Home Winning Runs In 7th

Al Kaline's single produced the go-ahead runs as Mickey Lolich won his 2nd game of the series for Detroit.

AL KALINE
Outfield
TIGERS

FRED LASHER
Pitcher
TIGERS

The Sporting News
1968 WORLD SERIES SPECIAL
LOLICH SERIES HERO
OUTDUELS GIBSON
Mickey Wins His 3rd Game

After six scoreless frames, Mickey and his mates broke through to wrap up the 1968 World Series.

MICKEY LOLICH
Pitcher
TIGERS

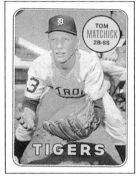

TOM MATCHICK
2B-SS
TIGERS

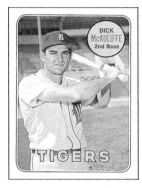

DICK McAULIFFE
2nd Base
TIGERS

DENNY McLAIN
Pitcher
TIGERS

The Sporting News
DENNY McLAIN
Pitcher
TIGERS
AMERICAN LEAGUE ALL-STARS

DON McMAHON
Pitcher
TIGERS

JIM NORTHRUP
Outfield
TIGERS

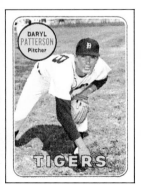

DARYL PATTERSON
Pitcher
TIGERS

JIM PRICE
Catcher
TIGERS

DICK RADATZ
Pitcher
TIGERS

JOE SPARMA
Pitcher
TIGERS

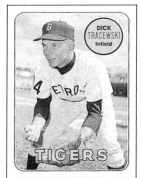

1968 WORLD SERIES SPECIAL

TIGER HOMERS
DECK THE CARDS

Horton, Cash & Lolich Connect

Willie Horton socked his home run in the 2nd inning.
Lolich hit his first homer ever in the next frame.

1968 WORLD SERIES SPECIAL

TIGER 10-RUN
INNING TIES MARK

Northrup Hits Grand-Slammer

Jim Northrup's bases loaded home run off Larry Jaster
topped 10-run Detroit rally in 3rd inning of Game #6.

★ The Sporting News ★

1968 WORLD SERIES SPECIAL

TIGERS CELEBRATE
THEIR VICTORY

Detroit's Heroes Go Wild

Detroit's Dick McAuliffe, Denny McLain and Willie Horton spent happy times after winning 1968 World Series.

1970

Two years after Denny McLain was on top of the world, he was now in the pits. He was suspended three times, the big one being from the beginning of the season until July 1 for allegedly participating in a bookmaking operation in 1967 and being involved with mobsters. He also had shorter suspensions for throwing a bucket of ice water on two reporters and for carrying a gun. In all, McLain was in uniform for only 58 games. He had a 3-5 record. After the season, the Tigers solved their problem by dealing him to Washington. Without McLain and with an ineffective Mickey Lolich (14-19), the Tigers dropped to fourth at 79-83, 29 games behind Baltimore. Mayo Smith was fired after the season. The Tigers were last in batting at .238. Injuries to Bill Freehan and Willie Horton limited each to fewer than 400 at-bats. Shortstop Cesar Gutierrez, who had only 20 hits going into the season, became the first American Leaguer to go seven-for-seven in a game, doing it in a 12-inning contest against Cleveland. He hit .243 for the season.

Gates Brown — OUTFIELD

Ike Brown — 2ND BASE

Norm Cash — 1ST BASE

Bill Freehan — CATCHER

THE SPORTING NEWS
BILL FREEHAN — C

Cesar Gutierrez — SHORTSTOP

John Hiller — PITCHER

Willie Horton — OUTFIELD

Dalton Jones | 1B-3B

Al Kaline | 1B-OF

Mike Kilkenny | PITCHER

Fred Lasher | PITCHER

Mickey Lolich | PITCHER

Dick McAuliffe | 2ND BASE

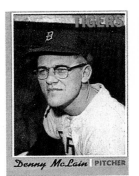
Denny McLain | PITCHER

The Sporting News ALL STAR
DENNY McLAIN — RHP

Jim Northrup | OUTFIELD

Daryl Patterson | PITCHER

Jimmie Price | CATCHER

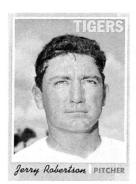
Jerry Robertson | PITCHER

Mayo Smith | MANAGER

Mickey Stanley | SS-OF

Tom Timmermann | PITCHER

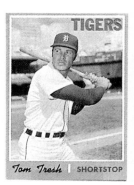
Tom Tresh | SHORTSTOP

Don Wert — 3RD BASE

Earl Wilson — PITCHER

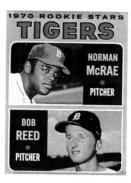

1970 ROOKIE STARS TIGERS — NORMAN McRAE PITCHER — BOB REED PITCHER

DETROIT TIGERS

1971

Billy Martin was the new manager and his main move was giving the ball to Mickey Lolich. The southpaw started an incredible 45 times, completing 29. His 376 innings pitched were the most by a major league since Grover Alexander pitched 388 in 1917. Lolich led the majors in wins with his 25-14 record and he became the first Tiger to get 300 strikeouts (308). His ERA was 2.92. The Tigers also had another 20-game winner in Joe Coleman (20-9, 3.15 ERA), who came to the Tigers in the Denny McLain trade. Detroit also obtained shortstop Ed Brinkman and third baseman Aurelio Rodriguez in that deal and they solidified the left side of the infield. The right side of the infield was strengthened by Norm Cash (tied for second in the league with 32 homers), who won the A.L. Comeback Player of the Year award for the second time (also in 1965). With seven Tigers hitting at least 15 homers, the team led the majors in homers with 179. All this added up to the Tigers' jumping into second place with a 91-71 record, 12 games behind Baltimore.

TIGERS
ed brinkman • shortstop

TIGERS
ike brown • 2nd base

TIGERS
gates brown • outfield

TIGERS
les cain • pitcher

TIGERS — norm cash • 1st base

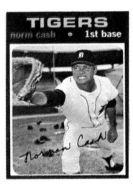

TIGERS — joe coleman • pitcher

TIGERS — kevin collins • infield

TIGERS — bill freehan • catcher

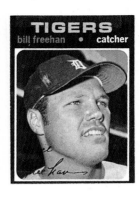

TIGERS — cesar gutierrez • ss

TIGERS — jim hannan • pitcher

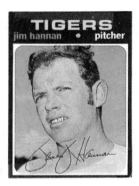

TIGERS — john hiller • pitcher

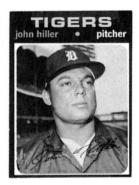

TIGERS — willie horton • outfield

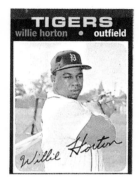

TIGERS — dalton jones • infield

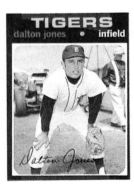

TIGERS — al kaline • outfield-1b

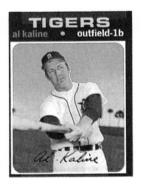

TIGERS — mike kilkenny • pitcher

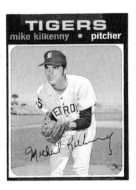

TIGERS — mickey lolich • pitcher

TIGERS — billy martin • manager

TIGERS — dick mc auliffe • 2b

TIGERS — russ nagelson • 1b-of

TIGERS — joe niekro • pitcher

TIGERS — jim northrup • outfield

TIGERS — daryl patterson • pitcher

TIGERS — jimmie price • catcher
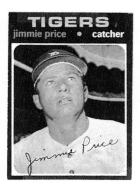

TIGERS — bob reed • pitcher

TIGERS — aurelio rodriguez • 3b
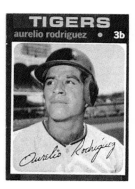

TIGERS — fred scherman • pitcher

TIGERS — mickey stanley • outfield

TIGERS — ken szotkiewicz • infield

TIGERS — tom timmermann • p
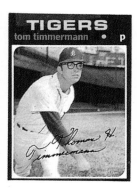

1971 ROOKIE STARS
TIGERS
terrin lagrow • pitcher
gene lamont • catcher

1971 ROOKIE STARS
TIGERS
dennis saunders • pitcher
tim marting • 2b shortstop
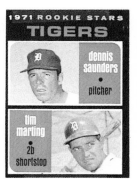

TIGERS

1972

Detroit trailed Boston by a half game going into the final series of the season. When the Tigers won the first two games behind the pitching of Mickey Lolich and Woodie Fryman, they were A.L. East champs. Detroit, which went 14-5 from Sept. 12 to Oct. 3, lost the final game on Oct. 4 so, with an 86-70 record, they finished a half game in front of Boston (85-70). The difference in games played occurred because a players' strike forced the opening of the season to be postponed until April 15 and the Red Sox had seven games canceled and the Tigers six. In the playoffs, Billy Martin's club lost three games to two to the A's. Lolich (22-14, 2.50 ERA) and Joe Coleman (19-14, 2.80 ERA), who won five games in September, received help down the stretch from Fryman. The lefthander was bought from the Phils on Aug. 2 and went 10-3 with a 2.05 ERA for the Tigers. Another late-season buy, catcher Duke Sims (Aug. 4 from the Dodgers), also gave the team a boost by hitting .316 while filling in for injured Bill Freehan. Al Kaline, in only 278 at-bats, hit .313, his highest average since 1961. Ed Brinkman, playing all 156 games, went 72 games without an error at shortstop and made only seven errors all season.

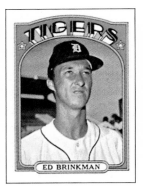

ED BRINKMAN

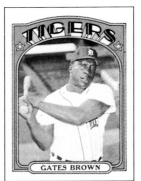

GATES BROWN

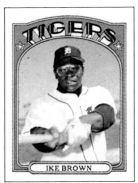

IKE BROWN

LES CAIN

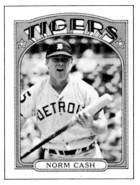

NORM CASH

JOE COLEMAN

BILL FREEHAN

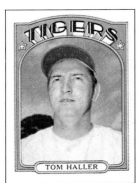

TOM HALLER

TOM HALLER
IN ACTION

BOYHOOD PHOTOS OF THE STARS

WILLIE HORTON

TIGERS
WILLIE HORTON

TIGERS
DALTON JONES

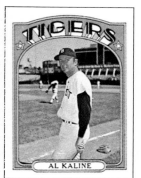

TIGERS
AL KALINE

TIGERS
MIKE KILKENNY

TIGERS
MICKEY LOLICH

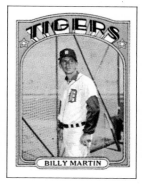

TIGERS
BILLY MARTIN

BILLY MARTIN
IN ACTION

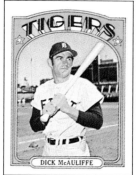

TIGERS
DICK McAULIFFE

TIGERS
JOE NIEKRO

TIGERS
JIM NORTHRUP

TIGERS
RON PERRANOSKI

TIGERS
AURELIO RODRIGUEZ

TIGERS
FRED SCHERMAN

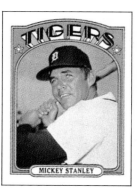

TIGERS
MICKEY STANLEY

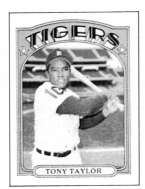
TONY TAYLOR

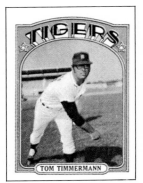
TOM TIMMERMANN

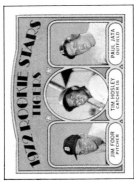

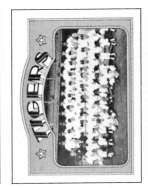

1973

On Aug. 13, the Tigers were 1½ games in front. After losing the last eight of 12 games on a road trip, they were six games behind. A week later, GM Jim Campbell, fed up that Billy Martin's personal business kept Martin away from the park too often, fired him. Coach Joe Schultz finished the season as Detroit manager (and Martin finished as Texas manager, being hired on Sept. 8). The Tigers wound up with an 85-77 record, in third place, 12 games behind Baltimore. Joe Coleman went 23-15, but lost seven in a row between Aug. 9 and Sept. 3. Mickey Lolich, the first $100,000 pitcher in Tiger history, had a 16-15 record and Jim Perry, obtained from Minnesota during spring training, went 14-13. The most amazing story belonged to John Hiller. The lefthanded reliever had suffered a heart attack in January 1971 and didn't pitch that season. He went 1-2 in 1972, but in 1973 was the A.L. Comeback player of the Year for going 10-5 with 38 saves and a 1.44 ERA.

ED
BRINKMAN
DETROIT TIGERS   SHORTSTOP

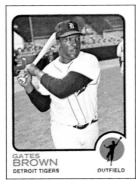
GATES
BROWN
DETROIT TIGERS   OUTFIELD

IKE
BROWN
DETROIT TIGERS   OUTFIELD

NORM
CASH
DETROIT TIGERS   1st BASE

JOE
COLEMAN
DETROIT TIGERS · PITCHER

CATCHER
BILL
FREEHAN
DETROIT TIGERS

WOODIE
FRYMAN
DETROIT TIGERS · PITCHER

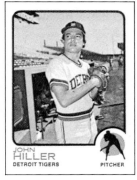

JOHN
HILLER
DETROIT TIGERS · PITCHER

WILLIE
HORTON
DETROIT TIGERS · OUTFIELD

FRANK
HOWARD
DETROIT TIGERS · 1st BASE

AL
KALINE
DETROIT TIGERS · OUTFIELD

LERRIN
LaGROW
DETROIT TIGERS · PITCHER

MICKEY
LOLICH
DETROIT TIGERS · PITCHER

COACHES
ART FOWLER
CHARLIE SILVERA
DICK TRACEWSKI

MANAGER
BILLY
MARTIN
DETROIT TIGERS

DICK
McAULIFFE
DETROIT TIGERS · 2nd BASE

JOE
NIEKRO
DETROIT TIGERS · PITCHER

JIM
NORTHRUP
DETROIT TIGERS · OUTFIELD

AURELIO
RODRIGUEZ
DETROIT TIGERS · 3rd BASE

FRED
SCHERMAN
DETROIT TIGERS · PITCHER

CHUCK
SEELBACH
DETROIT TIGERS · PITCHER

DUKE
SIMS
DETROIT TIGERS   CATCHER

BILL
SLAYBACK
DETROIT TIGERS   PITCHER

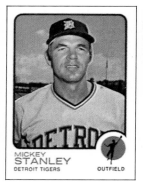

MICKEY
STANLEY
DETROIT TIGERS   OUTFIELD

TONY
TAYLOR
DETROIT TIGERS   2nd BASE

TOM
TIMMERMANN
DETROIT TIGERS   PITCHER

CHRIS
ZACHARY
DETROIT TIGERS   PITCHER

DETROIT TIGERS

1974

Al Kaline became the 12th player in history to reach 3,000 hits when he singled off Dave McNally. Kaline got seven more hits to end his 22-year Tiger career with 3,007. With a .297 lifetime average, he was the first 3,000-hit man to finish below .300. His 399 homers make Kaline the Tigers' all-time home run leader. It also was the last season for Detroit's No. 2 home run hitter. Norm Cash (377 homers), the regular first baseman since 1960, was released on Aug. 7. On that same day the Tigers sold Jim Northrup as they decided to go with youth. The Tigers were going nowhere but to last place — for only the second time in their 74-year tenure in the A.L. They were 43-37 on July 5, but went 29-63 the rest of the way to finish 72-90, 19 games behind Baltimore, in Ralph Houk's first season as manager. Mickey Lolich (16-21) became the first Tiger 20-game loser since Hooks Dauss in 1920. One of the few pleasant notes was John Hiller's setting a league record for wins by a reliever with 17.

DETROIT SHORTSTOP

ED BRINKMAN **TIGERS**

DETROIT DES. HITTER

GATES BROWN **TIGERS**

DETROIT 3B-OF

IKE BROWN **TIGERS**

DETROIT 1st BASE

NORM CASH **TIGERS**

DETROIT PITCHER

JOE COLEMAN **TIGERS**

DETROIT CATCHER

BOB DIDIER **TIGERS**

DETROIT PITCHER

ED FARMER **TIGERS**

DETROIT CATCHER

BILL FREEHAN **TIGERS**

DETROIT PITCHER

WOODIE FRYMAN **TIGERS**

DETROIT PITCHER

JOHN HILLER **TIGERS**

DETROIT OUTFIELD
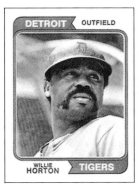
WILLIE HORTON **TIGERS**

DETROIT MANAGER
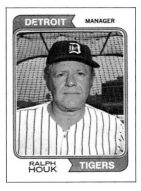
RALPH HOUK **TIGERS**

DETROIT 1B-OF

AL KALINE **TIGERS**

DETROIT PITCHER

LERRIN LaGROW **TIGERS**

DETROIT PITCHER

MICKEY LOLICH **TIGERS**

DETROIT OUTFIELD

JIM NORTHRUP **TIGERS**

DETROIT PITCHER
JIM PERRY
TIGERS

JIM RAY PITCHER
TRADED
TO DETROIT TIGERS

DETROIT 3rd BASE
AURELIO RODRIGUEZ
TIGERS

DETROIT PITCHER
FRED SCHERMAN
TIGERS

DETROIT PITCHER
CHUCK SEELBACH
TIGERS

DETROIT OUTFIELD
DICK SHARON
TIGERS

DETROIT OUTFIELD
MICKEY STANLEY
TIGERS

GARY SUTHERLAND 2B-3B
TRADED
TO DETROIT TIGERS

LUKE WALKER PITCHER
TRADED
TO DETROIT TIGERS

DETROIT TIGERS

1975

The Tigers were the worst team in the majors with their 57-102 record, which left them in last place in the A.L. East, 37½ games behind Boston. The Tigers went 11-47 from July 29 on, starting this stretch by setting a club record of 19 consecutive losses. With 173 errors, the Tigers committed their most since 1944. Joe Coleman fell to 10-18 with a 5.55 ERA in 201 innings. Mickey Lolich went 12-18 with a 3.77 ERA and after the season was traded to the Mets for Rusty Staub in a four-player deal. John Hiller had 14 saves and a 2.15 ERA but missed the last two months because of an injury. Willie Horton, now the team's designated hitter, won the Tigers' triple crown with 25 homers, 92 RBIs and a .275 average.

ED BRINKMAN

GATES BROWN

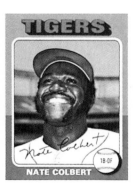
NATE COLBERT

JOE COLEMAN

BILL FREEHAN

WOODIE FRYMAN

JOHN HILLER

FRED HOLDSWORTH

WILLIE HORTON

'74 Highlights

KALINE JOINS 3000 HIT CLUB

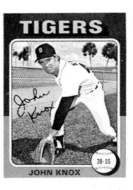

JOHN KNOX

LERRIN LaGROW

GENE LAMONT

RON LeFLORE

DAVE LEMANCZYK

MICKEY LOLICH

JERRY MOSES

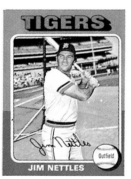

JIM NETTLES

BEN OGLIVIE

JIM RAY

AURELIO RODRIQUEZ

DICK SHARON

MICKEY STANLEY

GARY SUTHERLAND

LUKE WALKER

1976

The Bird was the word in baseball. Mark Fidrych, nicknamed The Bird after the Sesame Street character, was a crowd-pleasing rookie pitcher who talked to the ball, encouraged his teammates and baffled opposing batters. The exuberant righthander, who turned 22 that summer, hardly pitched in the first month. Not until May 15 did he win his first game. Then he kept winning, going to a 19-9 record and posting a major league-leading ERA of 2.34. He was the A.L.'s Rookie of the Year. His pitching was the main reason the fifth-place Tigers were the most improved team in the majors (17 more wins than in 1975) as they went 74-87, finishing 24 games behind the Yankees. However, there were others, too. Centerfielder Ron LeFlore stole 58 bases, the first Tiger to get more than 30 steals since Ty Cobb in 1918. LeFlore had the majors' longest hitting streak at 30 and hit .316, fifth best in the league. Rightfielder Rusty Staub had 96 RBIs (he was the only Tiger with more than 60) and batted .299. First baseman Jason Thompson hit 17 homers, the most by a Tiger rookie since Rudy York belted 35 in 1937.

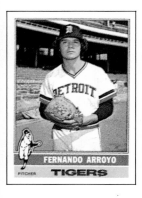

FERNANDO ARROYO
PITCHER **TIGERS**

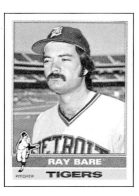

RAY BARE
PITCHER **TIGERS**

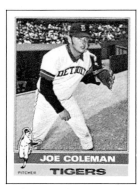

JOE COLEMAN
PITCHER **TIGERS**

DEC. 6 SPORTS EXTRA 1975
BENGALS GET CATFISH FROM ASTROS
PITCHER **JIM CRAWFORD**

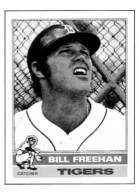

BILL FREEHAN
CATCHER
TIGERS

JOHN HILLER
PITCHER
TIGERS

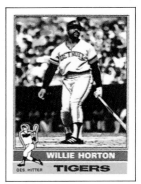

WILLIE HORTON
DES. HITTER
TIGERS

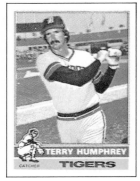

TERRY HUMPHREY
CATCHER
TIGERS

JOHN KNOX
THIRD BASE
TIGERS

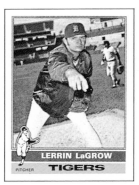

LERRIN LaGROW
PITCHER
TIGERS

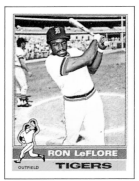

RON LeFLORE
OUTFIELD
TIGERS

DAVE LEMANCZYK
PITCHER
TIGERS

'75 RECORD BREAKER
MICKEY LOLICH
DETROIT TIGERS
★ MOST STRIKEOUTS, LIFETIME, LEFTHANDER—2,679

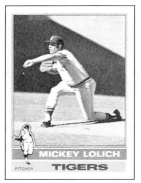

MICKEY LOLICH
PITCHER
TIGERS

DEC. 6 SPORTS EXTRA 1975
CATCHER MILT MAY DEALT TO BENGALS
CATCHER   MILT MAY

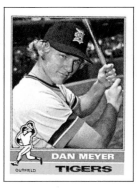

DAN MEYER
OUTFIELD
TIGERS

BEN OGLIVIE
OUTFIELD
TIGERS

JACK PIERCE
FIRST BASE
TIGERS

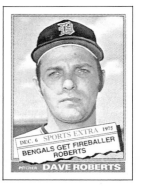

DEC. 6 SPORTS EXTRA 1975
BENGALS GET FIREBALLER ROBERTS
PITCHER   DAVE ROBERTS

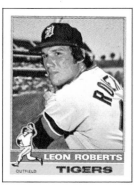

LEON ROBERTS
OUTFIELD
TIGERS

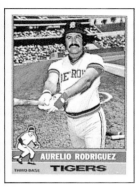

AURELIO RODRIGUEZ
THIRD BASE **TIGERS**

VERN RUHLE
PITCHER **TIGERS**

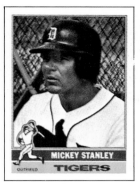

MICKEY STANLEY
OUTFIELD **TIGERS**

DEC. 12 SPORTS EXTRA 1975
LE GRAND ORANGE GOES
TO MOTOR CITY
OUTFIELD **RUSTY STAUB**

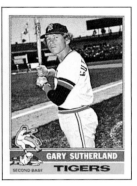

GARY SUTHERLAND
SECOND BASE **TIGERS**

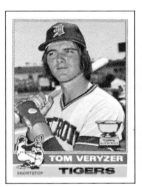

TOM VERYZER
SHORTSTOP **TIGERS**

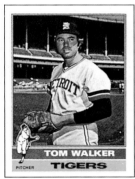

TOM WALKER
PITCHER **TIGERS**

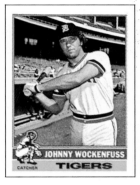

JOHNNY WOCKENFUSS
CATCHER **TIGERS**

≡1977≡

As quickly as The Bird appeared, that's almost how fast he disappeared. Two injuries brought him to earth, much to baseball's chagrin. He tore cartilage in his right knee during spring training and didn't make his first start until May 27. He went 6-4 in six weeks before tendinitis sidelined him for the season. Fidrych's arm never recovered and he won only four more games in his career. Another rookie, Dave Rozema, became the ace of the staff, going 15-7 with a 3.10 ERA. Steve Foucault, obtained from Texas in April for Willie Horton, replaced John Hiller as the team's top reliever with 13 saves and seven wins. Ron LeFlore became the first Tiger since Al Kaline in 1955 to get more than 200 hits and score 100 runs in the same season. LeFlore was again fifth in the batting race, this time at .325. Tito Fuentes batted .309, tops for a Tiger second baseman since Charlie Gehringer hit .313 in 1940. The power was supplied by Jason Thompson (31 homers, 105 RBIs), DH Rusty Staub (22 homers, 101 RBIs) and rookie leftfielder Steve Kemp (18 homers, 88 RBIs). Despite this hitting, the Tigers could do no better than 74-88, finishing 26 games behind the Yankees in fourth place in the seven-team A.L. East (expansion team Toronto joined the division).

TIGERS PITCHER
RAY BARE
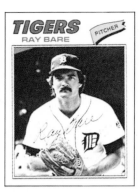

TIGERS PITCHER
JIM CRAWFORD

TIGERS PITCHER
MARK FIDRYCH

★ A.L. ALL-STARS ★

TIGERS CATCHER
BILL FREEHAN

TIGERS 2nd BASE
PEDRO GARCIA

TIGERS PITCHER
STEVE GRILLI
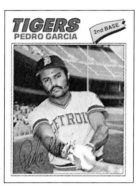

TIGERS PITCHER
JOHN HILLER

TIGERS DES. HITTER
WILLIE HORTON

TIGERS OUTFIELD
ALEX JOHNSON
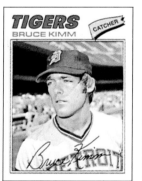

TIGERS CATCHER
BRUCE KIMM

TIGERS OUTFIELD
RON LeFLORE
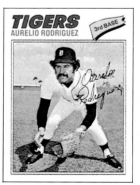
★ A.L. ALL-STARS ★

TIGERS CATCHER
MILT MAY
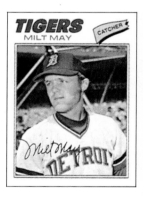

TIGERS OUTFIELD
BEN OGLIVIE

TIGERS PITCHER
DAVE ROBERTS

TIGERS 3rd BASE
AURELIO RODRIGUEZ

TIGERS PITCHER
VERN RUHLE

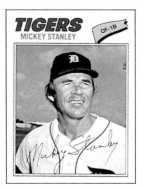

1978

The Tigers started off 17-6 through May 7 then played one game under .500 the rest of the way to finish 86-76. But in the strong A.L. East that was good for just fifth place as they finished 13½ games behind the Yankees. Ralph Houk retired after the season. What the Tigers finally found was a keystone combination that would be around for a decade. Second baseman Lou Whitaker (.285) was the A.L. Rookie Of The Year and Alan Trammell (.268) was a talented rookie shortstop. Ron LeFlore (.297) led the majors in runs (126) and the A.L. in steals (68). Rusty Staub was the league's best DH and his 121 RBIs were second in the majors to Jim Rice's 139. Jason Thompson had another fine season (.287, 26 homers, 96 RBIs). Two pitchers obtained in trades in the offseason became the big winners: Jim Slaton (from Milwaukee) went 17-11 and Jack Billingham (from Cincinnati) 15-8. After the season Slaton became a free agent and returned to Milwaukee.

Tigers — FERNANDO ARROYO

Tigers — TIM CORCORAN

Tigers — MARK FIDRYCH

Tigers — STEVE FOUCAULT

Tigers — TITO FUENTES

Tigers — RORIC HARRISON

Tigers — JOHN HILLER

Tigers — RALPH HOUK · AS MANAGER · AS PLAYER

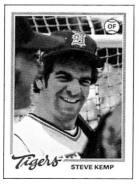

Tigers — STEVE KEMP

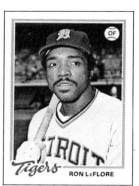

Tigers — RON LeFLORE

Tigers — PHIL MANKOWSKI

Tigers — MILT MAY

Tigers — BEN OGLIVIE

Tigers — AURELIO RODRIGUEZ

Tigers — DAVE ROZEMA

Tigers — VERN RUHLE

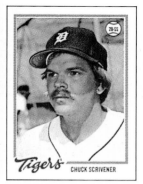
CHUCK SCRIVENER

MICKEY STANLEY

RUSTY STAUB

JASON THOMPSON

TOM VERYZER

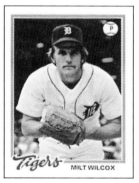
MILT WILCOX

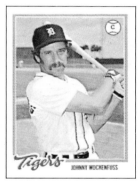
JOHNNY WOCKENFUSS

1979

Les Moss, manager of Evansville, succeeded Ralph Houk, but he didn't last long. He was fired June 12 with the Tigers at 27-26. His replacement was Sparky Anderson, who surprisingly had been fired as Cincinnati manager during the offseason. The Tigers lost nine of their first 11 games under Anderson before straightening out. They finished 85-76, but that still meant fifth place, 18 games behind Baltimore. Steve Kemp, in only 134 games, won the Tiger triple crown, leading the team in batting (.318), homers (26) and RBIs (105). Ron LeFlore stole 78 bases, hit .300 and became the first Tiger to score 100 runs three straight years since Hank Greenberg. After the season he was traded to Montreal. Jack Morris, despite spending the first month in the minors, led the Tigers with a 17-7 record and his 3.27 ERA was fifth best in the league. Aurelio Lopez, obtained from the Cards in the offseason, went 10-4 with 21 saves under Anderson (he was 0-1, no saves before him). Rusty Staub, a holdout who did not report until May 1, hit only .236 in 68 games and was traded to Montreal.

JACK BILLINGHAM P
TIGERS

TIM CORCORAN OF-DH
TIGERS

STEVE DILLARD 2B-SS
TIGERS

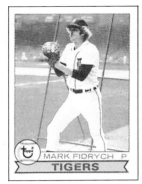

MARK FIDRYCH P
TIGERS

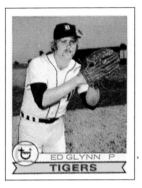

ED GLYNN P
TIGERS

JOHN HILLER P
TIGERS

STEVE KEMP OF
TIGERS

RON LeFLORE OF
TIGERS

PHIL MANKOWSKI 3B
TIGERS

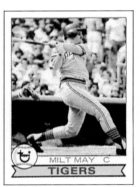

MILT MAY C
TIGERS

JACK MORRIS P
TIGERS

LANCE PARRISH C
TIGERS

AURELIO RODRIGUEZ 3B
TIGERS

DAVE ROZEMA P
TIGERS

JIM SLATON P
TIGERS

MICKEY STANLEY OF-1B
TIGERS

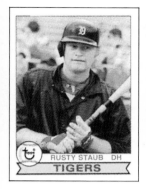

RUSTY STAUB   DH
TIGERS

BOB SYKES   P
TIGERS

JASON THOMPSON   1B
TIGERS

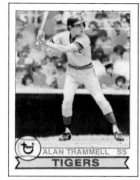

ALAN TRAMMELL   SS
TIGERS

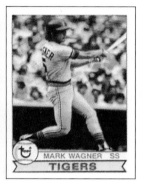

MARK WAGNER   SS
TIGERS

LOU WHITAKER   2B
TIGERS

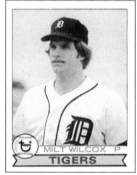

MILT WILCOX   P
TIGERS

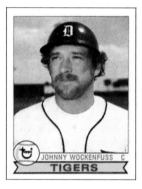

JOHNNY WOCKENFUSS   C
TIGERS

TIGERS   1979   PROSPECTS
KIP YOUNG   PITCHER
DAVE TOBIK   PITCHER
DAVE STEGMAN   OUTFIELD

TIGERS
LES MOSS   MANAGER

1980

Al Kaline became the tenth player voted into the Hall of Fame in his first year of eligibility. He had a better year than the Tigers. Though Detroit scored a major league high 830 runs, it could do no better than fifth place (84-78), 19 games behind the Yankees. Pitching was the problem. Dan Petry (10-9, 3.93 ERA) was the only starter with an ERA less than 4.00. Dan Schatzeder, obtained for Ron LeFlore, went 11-13 with a 4.01 ERA. Jack Morris was the top winner with 16, including a one-hitter of Minnesota, but he lost 15 and had a 4.18 ERA. Alan Trammell, moved into the second spot, hit .300 and scored 107 runs. Steve Kemp, despite injuries that limited him to 135 games, had 21 homers and 101 RBIs and hit .293. The Tigers traded Jason Thompson to the Angels for rightfielder Al Cowens because they wanted another righthanded bat. Cowens hit .280 for the Tigers to raise his average from .227 to .268.

PITCHER — JACK BILLINGHAM — TIGERS

3rd BASE — TOM BROOKENS — TIGERS

PITCHER — MARK FIDRYCH — TIGERS

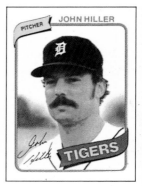

PITCHER — JOHN HILLER — TIGERS

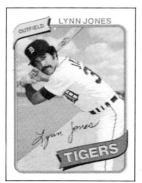

OUTFIELD — LYNN JONES — TIGERS

OUTFIELD — STEVE KEMP — TIGERS

OUTFIELD — RON LeFLORE — TIGERS

PITCHER — AURELIO LOPEZ — TIGERS

3rd BASE PHIL MANKOWSKI	OUTFIELD JERRY MORALES	PITCHER JACK MORRIS	CATCHER LANCE PARRISH
 TIGERS	 TIGERS	 TIGERS	 TIGERS

PITCHER DAN PETRY	C-1B EDDY PUTMAN	3rd BASE AURELIO RODRIGUEZ	PITCHER DAVE ROZEMA
 TIGERS	 TIGERS	 TIGERS	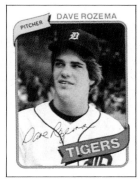 TIGERS

OUTFIELD CHAMP SUMMERS	1st BASE JASON THOMPSON	PITCHER DAVE TOBIK	SHORTSTOP ALAN TRAMMELL
 TIGERS	 TIGERS	 TIGERS	 TIGERS

PITCHER PAT UNDERWOOD	SHORTSTOP MARK WAGNER	2nd BASE LOU WHITAKER	PITCHER MILT WILCOX
 TIGERS	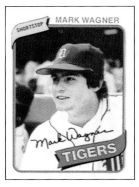 TIGERS	 TIGERS	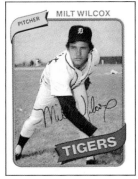 TIGERS

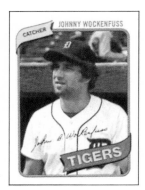
CATCHER JOHNNY WOCKENFUSS
TIGERS

PITCHER KIP YOUNG
TIGERS

FUTURE STARS
TIGERS
BRUCE ROBBINS PITCHER
AL GREENE OUTFIELD
MIKE CHRIS PITCHER

mgr SPARKY ANDERSON
TIGERS

1981

A 50-day players' strike caused the season to be divided into two halves. The Tigers went 31-26 in the first session, coming in fourth, 3½ games behind the Yankees. The Tigers had a chance to win the second half: they went into the final three-game series a half game behind Milwaukee but lost the first two games and were eliminated. They won the finale, to go 29-23, 1½ games behind the Brewers, in a tie for second with Boston. Kirk Gibson, a former Michigan State football star, was a key reason for the Tigers' run for first. A .234 hitter before the strike, he batted .375 after it. The Tigers also had terrific fielding, committing the fewest errors in the majors (67). Detroit received improved performances from Jack Morris (14-7, 3.05 ERA), Milt Wilcox (12-9, 3.04) and Dan Petry (10-9, 3.00). Kevin Saucier, in his first year with Detroit, was a major surprise, becoming the bullpen stopper (4-2, 1.65 ERA, 13 saves). Steve Kemp was traded after the season to the White Sox for centerfielder Chet Lemon.

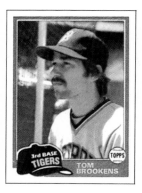
3rd BASE TIGERS
TOM BROOKENS
TOPPS

OUTFIELD TIGERS
TIM CORCORAN
TOPPS

OUTFIELD TIGERS
AL COWENS
TOPPS

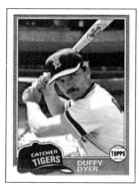
CATCHER TIGERS
DUFFY DYER
TOPPS

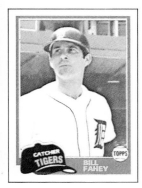

CATCHER
TIGERS
BILL
FAHEY

PITCHER
TIGERS
MARK
FIDRYCH

OUTFIELD
TIGERS
KIRK
GIBSON

1st BASE
TIGERS
RICH
HEBNER

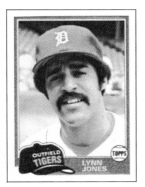

OUTFIELD
TIGERS
LYNN
JONES

3B-SS
TIGERS
MICK
KELLEHER

OUTFIELD
TIGERS
STEVE
KEMP

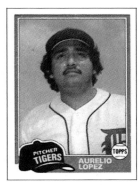

PITCHER
TIGERS
AURELIO
LOPEZ

PITCHER
TIGERS
JACK
MORRIS

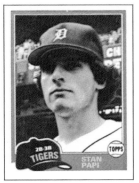

2B-3B
TIGERS
STAN
PAPI

CATCHER
TIGERS
LANCE
PARRISH

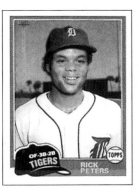

OF-3B-2B
TIGERS
RICK
PETERS

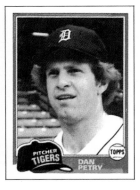

PITCHER
TIGERS
DAN
PETRY

PITCHER
TIGERS
BRUCE
ROBBINS

PITCHER
TIGERS
DAVE
ROZEMA

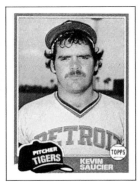

PITCHER
TIGERS
KEVIN
SAUCIER

PITCHER TIGERS — DAN SCHATZEDER

OUTFIELD TIGERS — CHAMP SUMMERS

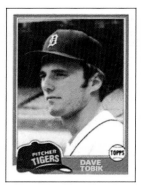

PITCHER TIGERS — DAVE TOBIK

SHORTSTOP TIGERS — ALAN TRAMMELL

PITCHER TIGERS — PAT UNDERWOOD

SHORTSTOP TIGERS — MARK WAGNER

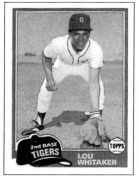

2nd BASE TIGERS — LOU WHITAKER

PITCHER TIGERS — MILT WILCOX

C-1B OF TIGERS — JOHNNY WOCKENFUSS

TIGERS FUTURE STARS — ROGER WEAVER PITCHER / JERRY UDUR PITCHER / DAVE STEFFEN PITCHER

DETROIT TIGERS — SPARKY ANDERSON, MANAGER

1982

The Tigers were in first place (34-18) on June 9 before going on a 2-15 streak, including 10 straight losses, which sent them into fourth. That's where they finished, 12 games behind Milwaukee with their 83-79 record. They lost 28 games from the seventh inning on. The bullpen was ineffective. Kevin Saucier lost his stuff and injuries ruined the seasons of Aurelio Lopez (sore shoulder) and Dave Rozema (torn knee ligaments in a brawl at Minnesota on May 14). However, with good starting pitching, the Tigers had the lowest ERA in the league (3.80). Jack Morris (17-16) and Dan Petry (15-9) were the two big winners. Lance Parrish (.284, 32 homers, 87 RBIs) established himself as the best catcher in the American League. Leftfielder Larry Herndon, acquired from the Giants for Dan Schatzeder, batted .292 with 23 homers and 88 RBIs. Kirk Gibson, beset by injuries, hit .278 with only eight homers in 266 at-bats.

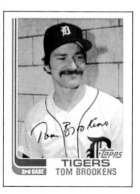

TIGERS
3rd BASE TOM BROOKENS

TIGERS
3B-SS ENOS CABELL

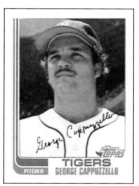

TIGERS
PITCHER GEORGE CAPPUZZELLO

TIGERS
OUTFIELD AL COWENS

TIGERS
CATCHER BILL FAHEY

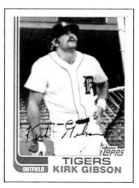

TIGERS
OUTFIELD KIRK GIBSON

TIGERS
1st BASE RICH HEBNER

TIGERS
OUTFIELD LARRY HERNDON

TIGERS
DES. HITTER MIKE IVIE

TIGERS
1st BASE RON JACKSON

TIGERS
OUTFIELD LYNN JONES

TIGERS
3B-SS MICK KELLEHER

TIGERS
OUTFIELD STEVE KEMP

TIGERS
1st BASE RICK LEACH

TIGERS
OUTFIELD CHET LEMON

TIGERS
PITCHER AURELIO LOPEZ

TIGERS
PITCHER JACK MORRIS

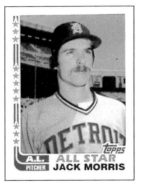

ALL STAR
A.L. PITCHER JACK MORRIS

TIGERS
2B-3B STAN PAPI

TIGERS
CATCHER LANCE PARRISH

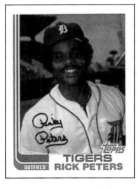

TIGERS
OUTFIELD RICK PETERS

TIGERS
PITCHER DAN PETRY

TIGERS
PITCHER DAVE ROZEMA

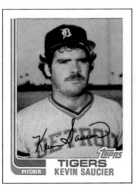

TIGERS
PITCHER KEVIN SAUCIER

TIGERS
PITCHER DAN SCHATZEDER

TIGERS
PITCHER ELIAS SOSA

TIGERS
OUTFIELD CHAMP SUMMERS

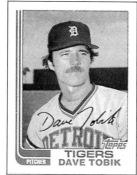

TIGERS
PITCHER DAVE TOBIK

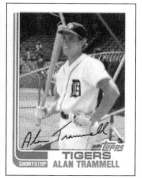

TIGERS
SHORTSTOP ALAN TRAMMELL

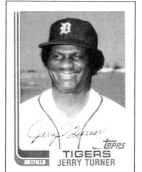

TIGERS
OUTFIELD JERRY TURNER

TIGERS
PITCHER PAT UNDERWOOD

TIGERS
2nd BASE LOU WHITAKER

TIGERS
PITCHER MILT WILCOX

TIGERS
C-1B-OF JOHNNY WOCKENFUSS

DETROIT TIGERS
'81 BATTING & PITCHING LDRS.

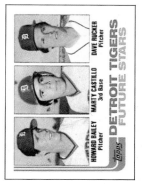

DETROIT TIGERS
FUTURE STARS

DAVE RUCKER
Pitcher

MARTY CASTILLO
3rd Base

HOWARD BAILEY
Pitcher

1983

The Tigers had their best record since they won the pennant in 1968. However, 92-70 still left them in second place, six games behind Baltimore. On April 15, Milt Wilcox retired the first 26 White Sox batters before pinch-hitter Jerry Hairston singled to break up the perfect game. He settled for the one-hit shutout. Jack Morris (20-13, 3.34 ERA) led the A.L. in strikeouts with 232 and became the first Tiger pitcher to win 20 games since Joe Coleman 10 years earlier. Dan Petry (19-11) failed in his bid for 20 games when he lost on the last day. Despite Kirk Gibson's hitting .227 in 401 at-bats, the Tigers' .274 team average was the third highest in baseball. Lou Whitaker (.320, third in the league) became the first lefthanded hitter to get 200 hits for the Tigers since Dick Wakefield in 1943. Alan Trammell (.319, fourth) became the first Tiger shortstop to get 30 steals since Donie Bush in 1917 and was the league's Comeback Player of the Year. Lance Parrish (27 homers, 114 RBIs) and Larry Herndon (.302, 20 homers, 92 RBIs) came through again. After the season, John Fetzer, 82, sold the team to pizza king Thomas Monaghan for a reported $43 million.

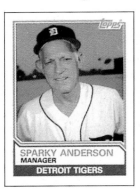

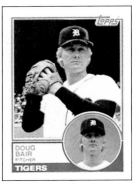

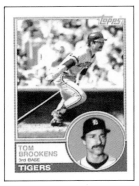

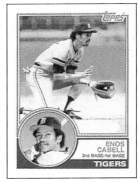

MIKE IVIE
DESIGNATED HITTER
TIGERS

LYNN
JONES
OUTFIELD
TIGERS

RICK
LEACH
1st BASE
TIGERS

CHET
LEMON
OUTFIELD
TIGERS

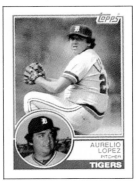

AURELIO
LOPEZ
PITCHER
TIGERS

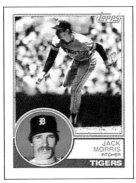

JACK
MORRIS
PITCHER
TIGERS

1982 RECORD BREAKER
Threw out 3 Baserunners in
All-Star Game to Set Record
LANCE PARRISH

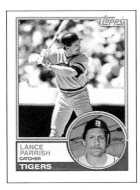

LANCE
PARRISH
CATCHER
TIGERS

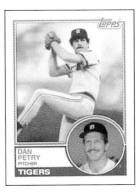

DAN PETRY
PITCHER
TIGERS

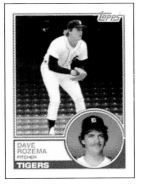

DAVE
ROZEMA
PITCHER
TIGERS

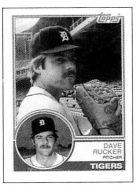

DAVE
RUCKER
PITCHER
TIGERS

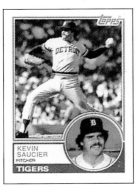

KEVIN
SAUCIER
PITCHER
TIGERS

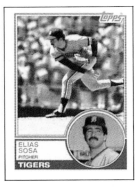

ELIAS
SOSA
PITCHER
TIGERS

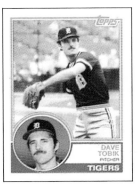

DAVE
TOBIK
PITCHER
TIGERS

ALAN
TRAMMELL
SHORTSTOP
TIGERS

JERRY
TURNER
OUTFIELD
TIGERS

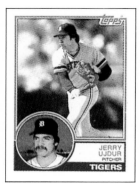

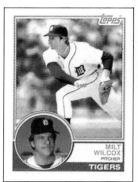

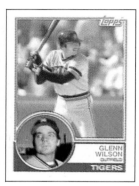

1984

The Tigers began by winning their first nine games and never slowed down. They were 35-5 on May 24 for the best 40-game start in history. They finished 104-58 (their most wins ever), 15 games ahead of Toronto. They swept the Royals in three games in the playoffs and beat the Padres in five games in the World Series for their first championship since 1968. They were the first team since the 1955 Dodgers to lead from start to finish. Sparky Anderson became the first manager to win 100 games in both leagues and the first to manage Series winners in both leagues. Lefthander reliever Willie Hernandez, obtained from Philadelphia in March, had 32 saves in 33 save opportunities, a 9-3 record and a 1.92 ERA. He was the league's MVP and Cy Young Award Winner. Jack Morris (19-11) pitched the first Tiger no-hitter since Jim Bunning in 1958 and started off 10-1 before cooling off. Dan Petry went 18-8 and Milt Wilcox 17-8. The Tigers led the majors with **829 runs and 187 homers. Major contributors were Kirk Gibson (.282, 27 homers, 91 RBIs, 29 steals, playoff MVP), Lance Parrish (33 homers, 98 RBIs) and Alan Trammell (.314, 69 RBIs, fourth Gold Glove, Series MVP). The Tigers drew their most fans ever (2,704,794).

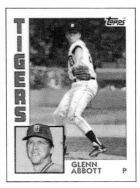

GLENN ABBOTT P

MANAGER
SPARKY ANDERSON

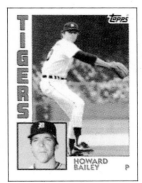

HOWARD BAILEY P

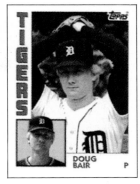

DOUG BAIR P

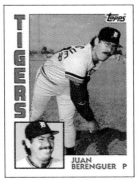

JUAN BERENGUER P

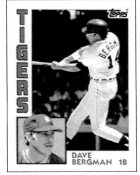

DAVE BERGMAN 1B

TOM BROOKENS 3B

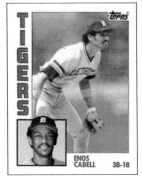

ENOS CABELL 3B-1B

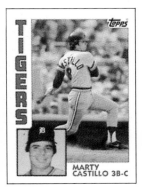

MARTY CASTILLO 3B-C

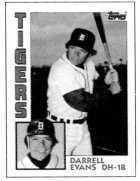

DARRELL EVANS DH-1B

BARBARO GARBEY 3B-1B

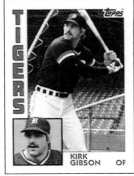

KIRK GIBSON OF

JOHNNY GRUBB OF

DAVE GUMPERT P

WILLIE HERNANDEZ P

LARRY HERNDON OF

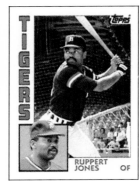
LYNN
JONES OF

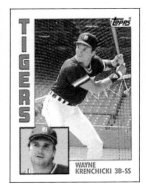
RUPPERT
JONES OF

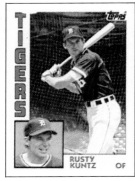
WAYNE
KRENCHICKI 3B-SS

RUSTY
KUNTZ OF

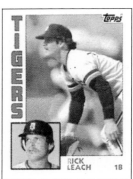
RICK
LEACH 1B

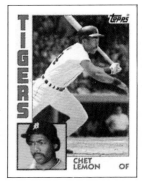
CHET
LEMON OF

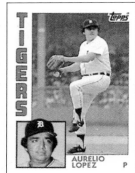
AURELIO
LOPEZ P

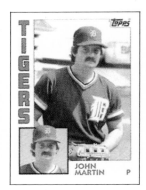
JOHN
MARTIN P

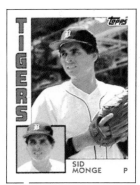
SID
MONGE P

JACK
MORRIS P

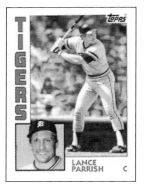
LANCE
PARRISH C

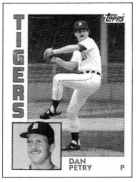
DAN
PETRY P

DAVE
ROZEMA P

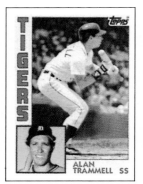
ALAN
TRAMMELL SS

LOU
WHITAKER 2B

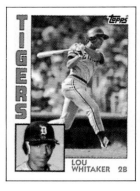
LOU
WHITAKER 2B

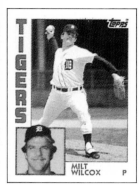

MILT WILCOX P

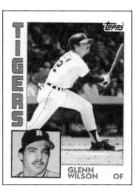

GLENN WILSON OF

JOHNNY WOCKENFUSS C-1B- OF

BATTING & PITCHING LEADERS

JACK MORRIS 3.34 ERA

LOU WHITAKER .320 BA

TIGERS

1985

The Tigers were in contention at 47-34 on July 10, but then went 37-43 in the second half to finish at 84-77, in third place, 15 games behind Toronto. Though Lou Whitaker and Lance Parrish won their third straight Gold Gloves, fielding was the Tigers' big problem as they committed 143 errors, the second most in the A.L. Leadoff man Whitaker also hit 21 homers and Parrish had 28 homers and 98 RBIs. But when it came to homers nobody did it better than Darrell Evans, who at 38 became the oldest player to lead the A.L. in homers (40). The first baseman-DH who signed as a free agent before the 1984 season, became the first Tiger home run champ since Hank Greenberg in 1946. Kirk Gibson put it together again (.287, 29 homers, 97 RBIs, 30 steals), but Larry Herndon didn't (.244). Willie Hernandez was effective (31 saves, 2.70 ERA, 8-10) though not untouchable.

TIGERS MANAGER
SPARKY ANDERSON

TIGERS P
DOUG BAIR

TIGERS 2B
DOUG BAKER

TIGERS P
JUAN BERENGUER

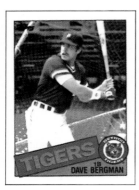

TIGERS
1B
DAVE BERGMAN

TIGERS
3B
TOM BROOKENS

TIGERS
C
MARTY CASTILLO

TIGERS
DH-1B
DARRELL EVANS

TIGERS
3B-1B
BARBARO GARBEY

TIGERS
OF
KIRK GIBSON

TIGERS
OF
JOHNNY GRUBB

TIGERS
P
WILLIE HERNANDEZ

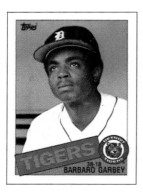

TIGERS
OF
LARRY HERNDON

TIGERS
3B
HOWARD JOHNSON

TIGERS
OF
RUPPERT JONES

TIGERS
OF
RUSTY KUNTZ

TIGERS
OF
CHET LEMON

TIGERS
P
AURELIO LOPEZ

TIGERS
P
SID MONGE

TIGERS
P
JACK MORRIS

LANCE PARRISH

LANCE PARRISH
CATCHER
AL ALL STAR

DAN PETRY

DAVE ROZEMA

BILL SCHERRER

ALAN TRAMMELL

LOU WHITAKER

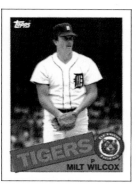

MILT WILCOX

1986

The Tigers set a team record with their ninth straight winning season. They won their last five games to finish in third place at 87-75, 8½ games behind the Red Sox. Their infield became the second in history to have each player hit 20 homers (the 1940 Red Sox were the first). Darrell Evans led the team with 29 homers, Alan Trammell hit a career-high 21, and Lou Whitaker and third baseman Darnell Coles, obtained from Seattle in the offseason, had 20. Kirk Gibson, though limited to 119 games because of a severe ankle injury, hit 28 homers and Lance Parrish, who missed the last two months with a back injury, had 22 as the Tigers led the majors with 198 dingers. Trammell led the regulars with a .277 average, scored 107 runs and knocked in a career-high 75. Gibson tied for the team lead in RBIs with Coles (86) and stole a team-high 34 bases. Jack Morris led the majors in shutouts (six) and tied for second in victories as he went 21-8 with a 3.27 ERA. Willie Hernandez led the team with 24 saves, most of them in the first half.

TIGERS

SPARKY ANDERSON

TIGERS

JUAN BERENGUER

TIGERS

DAVE BERGMAN

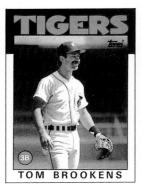

TIGERS

TOM BROOKENS

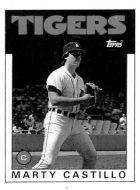

TIGERS

MARTY CASTILLO

TIGERS

DARRELL EVANS

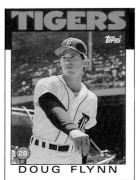

TIGERS

DOUG FLYNN

TIGERS

BARBARO GARBEY

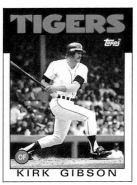

TIGERS

KIRK GIBSON

TIGERS

JOHNNY GRUBB

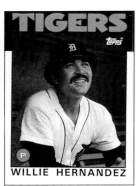

TIGERS

WILLIE HERNANDEZ

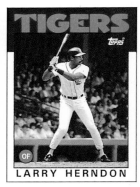

TIGERS

LARRY HERNDON

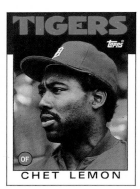

TIGERS

CHET LEMON

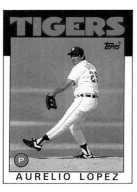

TIGERS

AURELIO LOPEZ

TIGERS

BOB MELVIN

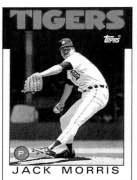

TIGERS

JACK MORRIS

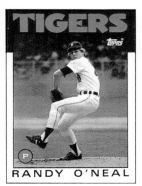

RANDY O'NEAL

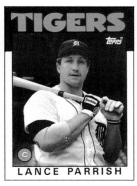

LANCE PARRISH

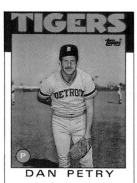

DAN PETRY

CHRIS PITTARO

CHRIS PITTARO

ALEJANDRO SANCHEZ

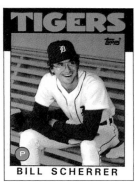

BILL SCHERRER

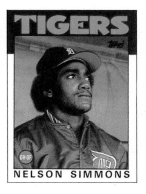

NELSON SIMMONS

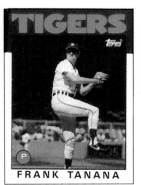

FRANK TANANA

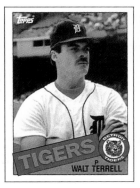

WALT TERRELL

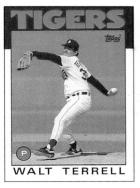

WALT TERRELL

ALAN TRAMMELL

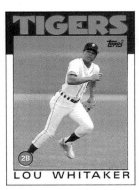

LOU WHITAKER

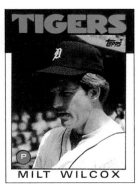

MILT WILCOX

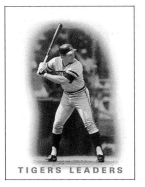

TIGERS LEADERS

SPARKY ANDERSON

DAVE BERGMAN

TOM BROOKENS

BILL CAMPBELL

CHUCK CARY

DARNELL COLES

DAVE COLLINS

DARRELL EVANS

1987

A lot of people were surprised when the Tigers emerged as the American League's East winner but Sparky Anderson wasn't one of them. The Detroit skipper spent much of the summer telling listeners not to count his ball club out, but there were a few times even the optimistic Anderson had to wonder.

His slumbering Tigers were eight games under .500 in mid-May, but once he got the lineup straightened out and big Kirk Gibson healthy, the Bengals moved into the race they finally captured in a stirring series with Toronto in the final week.

Detroit had five players with 20 or more homers, with veteran Darrell Evans leading the way with 34 four-baggers, plus 99 runs batted in. Alan Trammell's .343 average paced the club, as did his 105 RBIs. The shortstop also hit 28 homers. Rookie catcher Matt Nokes had 32 homers and 87 runs batted in. Chet Lemon hit 20 homers and drove in 75. Gibson, the club leader with 26 steals, banged two dozen homers and drove home 79.

Jack Morris (18-11), Walt Terrell (17-10) and Frank Tanana (15-10) gave the Tigers the nucleus of a winning rotation. But it was the August acquisition of righthander Doyle Alexander that finally made the difference. Alexander was 9-0 in 11 late-season starts and pitched to a nifty 1.53 ERA. As for what had been a shaky bullpen, rookie righthander Mike Henneman jumped in to win 11 games and save seven more.

KIRK GIBSON

JOHNNY GRUBB

MIKE HEATH

MIKE HENNEMAN

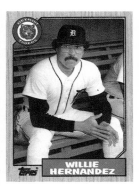

WILLIE HERNANDEZ

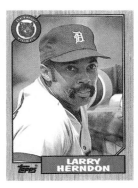

LARRY HERNDON

ERIC KING

CHET LEMON

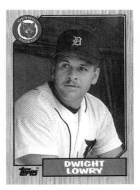

DWIGHT LOWRY

BILL MADLOCK

JACK MORRIS

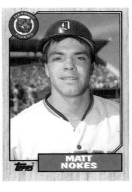

MATT NOKES

RANDY O'NEAL

LANCE PARRISH

LANCE PARRISH
ALL STAR

DAN PETRY

JEFF ROBINSON

BILL SCHERRER

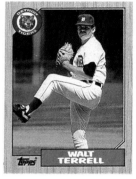

PAT SHERIDAN

JIM SLATON

FRANK TANANA

WALT TERRELL

MARK THURMOND

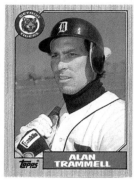

ALAN TRAMMELL

LOU WHITAKER

TIGERS LEADERS

1988

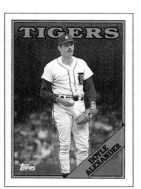

TIGERS
DOYLE ALEXANDER
Topps

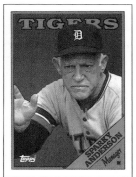

TIGERS
SPARKY ANDERSON
Manager
Topps

TIGERS
BILLY BEAN
Topps

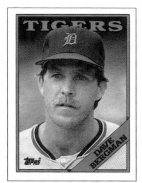

TIGERS
DAVE BERGMAN
Topps

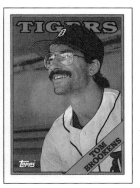

TIGERS
TOM BROOKENS
Topps

TIGERS
DARRELL EVANS
Topps

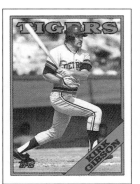

TIGERS
KIRK GIBSON
Topps

TIGERS
JOHNNY GRUBB
Topps

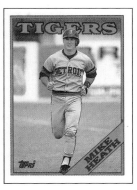

TIGERS
MIKE HEATH
Topps

TIGERS
MIKE HENNEMAN
Topps

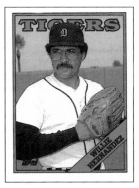

TIGERS
WILLIE HERNANDEZ
Topps

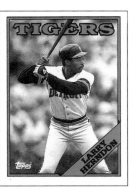

TIGERS
LARRY HERNDON
Topps

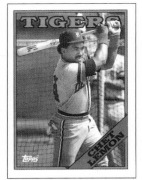

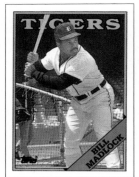

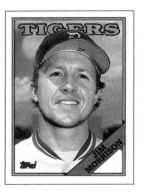

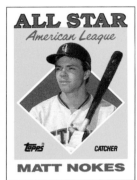

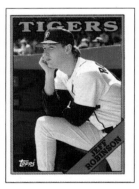

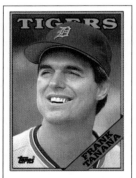

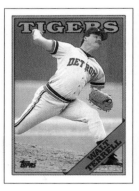

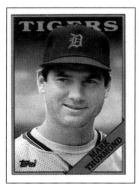

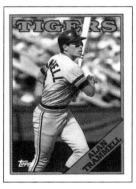

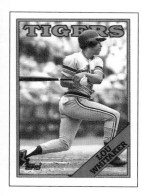

Salute To TY COBB

The Sporting News
ALL-TIME ALL-STARS

TY COBB OF

When Ty Cobb retired as an active player following the 1928 season, he held 43 various records for batting, base running and all-round durability and performance.

In the interim more than a few of his standards have been broken, but you can bet your bottom buck the .367 lifetime batting average he compiled in his 24 seasons will never be equaled, let alone surpassed.

Cobb is regarded by many, particularly in Detroit where he performed 22 seasons, as the finest ever to play the game. The first man elected to the Hall of Fame — he got an unprecedented 98% of the initial vote that produced five inductions — Tyrus Raymond's journey was pocked with stormy and argumentative moments. But the hot-blooded Georgian, whom the Tigers acquired at the age of 19 in 1905, never failed to leave an impression on the fans who crowded American League ballparks to view his unique performances.

Until the immortal Babe Ruth's home run bat began altering baseball in 1920, the game belonged to Cobb. It's still known as the Cobbian Era. He was its most singular performer and some of the numbers he created remain inviolate to this day.

For instance, no one ever hit .300 for 23 straight seasons as the Georgia Peach did from 1906 to 1928. Nor has anyone approached the dozen batting titles he won, including a record nine in a row from 1907 to 1915.

It wasn't until Pete Rose did it in 1985 that anyone surpassed Ty's long-standing mark of 4,191 career base hits. What's rarely mentioned about Rose's feat is the fact he had over 2,000 more at bats than Cobb before he erased the mark.

Arithmetic compiled by ballplayers often become cold statistics on the game's ledger sheets. As a result they are too often discarded after a cursory glance. However, what Cobb accomplished should not be lightly dismissed. His numbers should be required reading, particularly by current fans who are easily enthralled by something done by one of today's major leaguers.

In his time Cobb was among the best paid in the game, but even his top salaries pale against today's minimum. When one considers the contracts being offered to current major leaguers, it would be virtually impossible to estimate what a Ty Cobb would be worth on the present market.

He was the best, and whoever is in second place isn't even close.

1951: Blue Back of Johnny Mize (50) lists for $25 . . . Red Back of Duke Snider (38) lists for $18 . . . Complete set of 9 Team Cards lists for $900 . . . Complete set of 11 Connie Mack All-Stars lists for $2750 with Babe Ruth and Lou Gehrig listing for $700 each . . . Current All-Stars of Jim Konstanty, Robin Roberts and Eddie Stanky list for $4000 each . . . Complete set lists for $14,250.

1952: Mickey Mantle (311) is unquestionably the most sought-after post-war gum card, reportedly valued at $6,500-plus . . . Ben Chapman (391) is photo of Sam Chapman . . . Complete set lists in excess of $36,000.

1953: Mickey Mantle (82) and Willie Mays (244) list for $1,500 each . . . Set features first TOPPS card of Hall-of-Famer Whitey Ford (207) and only TOPPS card of Hall-of-Famer Satchel Paige (220). Pete Runnels (219) is photo of Don Johnson . . . Complete set lists for $9,500.

1954: Ted Williams is depicted on two cards (1 and 250) . . . Set features rookie cards of Hank Aaron (128), Ernie Banks (94) and Al Kaline (201) . . . Card of Aaron lists for $650 . . . Card of Willie Mays (90) lists for $200 . . . Complete set lists for $5,500.

1955: Set features rookie cards of Sandy Koufax (123), Harmon Killebrew (124) and Roberto Clemente (164) . . . The Clemente and Willie Mays (194) cards list for $425 each . . . Complete set lists for $3,900.

1956: Set features rookie cards of Hall-of-Famers Will Harridge (1), Warren Giles (2), Walter Alston (8) and Luis Aparicio (292) . . . Card of Mickey Mantle (135) lists for $650 . . . Card of Willie Mays (130) lists for $125 . . . Complete set lists for $4,000 . . . The Team Cards are found both dated (1955) and undated and are valued at $15 (dated) and more . . . There are two unnumbered Checklist Cards valued high.

1957: Set features rookie cards of Don Drysdale (18), Frank Robinson (35) and Brooks Robinson (328) . . . A reversal of photo negative made Hank Aaron (20) appear as a left-handed batter . . . Card of Mickey Mantle (95) lists for $600 . . . Cards of Brooks Robinson and Sandy Koufax (302) list for $275 each . . . Complete set lists for $4,800.

1958: Set features first TOPPS cards of Casey Stengel (475) and Stan Musial (476) . . . Mike McCormick (37) is photo of Ray Monzant . . . Milt Bolling (188) is photo of Lou Berberet . . . Bob Smith (226) is photo of Bobby Gene Smith . . . Card of Mickey Mantle (150) lists for $400 . . . Card of Ted Williams (1) lists for $325 . . . Complete set lists for $4,800.

1959: In a notable error, Lou Burdette (440) is shown posing as a left-handed pitcher . . . Set features rookie card of Bob Gibson (514) . . . Ralph Lumenti (316) is photo of Camilo Pascual . . . Card of Gibson lists for $200 . . . Card of Mickey Mantle (10) lists for $300 . . . Complete set lists for $3,000.

1960: A run of 32 consecutively numbered rookie cards (117-148) includes the first card of Carl Yastrzemski (148) . . . J.C. Martin (346) is photo of Gary Peters . . . Gary Peters (407) is photo of J.C. Martin . . . Card of Yastrzemski lists for $150 . . . Card of Mickey Mantle (350) lists for $300 . . . Complete set lists for $2,600.

1961: The Warren Spahn All-Star (589) should have been numbered 587 . . . Set features rookie cards of Billy Williams (141) and Juan Marichal (417) . . . Dutch Dotterer (332) is photo of his brother, Tommy . . . Card of Mickey Mantle (300) lists for $200 . . . Card of Carl Yastrzemski (287) lists for $90 . . . Complete set lists for $3,600.

1962: Set includes special Babe Ruth feature (135-144) . . . some Hal Reniff cards numbered 139 should be 159 . . . Set features rookie card of Lou Brock (387) . . . Gene Freese (205) is shown posing as a left-handed batter . . . Card of Mickey Mantle (200) lists for $325 . . . Card of Carl Yastrzemski (425) lists for $125 . . . Complete set lists for $3,300.

1963: Set features rookie card of Pete Rose (537), which lists for $500-plus . . . Bob Uecker (126) is shown posing as a left-handed batter . . . Don Landrum (113) is photo of Ron Santo . . . Eli Grba (231) is photo of Ryne Duren . . . Card of Mickey Mantle (200) lists for $200 . . . Card of Lou Brock (472) lists for $75 . . . Complete set lists for $2,900.

1964: Set features rookie cards of Richie Allen (243), Tony Conigliaro (287) and Phil Niekro (541) . . . Lou Burdette is again shown posing as a left-handed pitcher . . . Bud Bloomfield (532) is photo of Jay Ward . . . Card of Pete Rose (125) lists for $150 . . . Card of Mickey Mantle (50) lists for $175 . . . Complete set lists for $1,600.

1965: Set features rookie cards of Dave Johnson (473), Steve Carlton (477) and Jim Hunter (526) . . . Lew Krausse (462) is photo of Pete Lovrich . . . Gene Freese (492) is again shown posing as a left-handed batter . . . Cards of Carlton and Pete Rose (207) list for $135 . . . Card of Mickey Mantle (350) lists for $300 . . . Complete set lists for $800.

1966: Set features rookie card of Jim Palmer (126) . . . For the third time (see 1962 and 1965) Gene Freese (319) is shown posing as a left-handed batter . . . Dick Ellsworth (447) is photo of Ken Hubbs (died February 13, 1964) . . . Card of Gaylord Perry (598) lists for $175 . . . Card of Willie McCovey (550) lists for $80 . . . Complete set lists for $2,500.

1967: Set features rookie cards of Rod Carew (569) and Tom Seaver (581) . . . Jim Fregosi (385) is shown posing as a left-handed batter . . . George Korince (72) is photo of James Brown but was later corrected on a second Korince card (526) . . . Card of Carew lists for $150 . . . Card of Maury Wills (570) lists for $65 . . . Complete set lists for $2,500.

1968: Set features rookie cards of Nolan Ryan (177) and Johnny Bench (247) . . . The special feature of The Sporting News All-Stars (361-380) includes eight players in the Hall of Fame . . . Card of Ryan lists for $135 . . . Card of Bench lists for $125 . . . Complete set lists for $1,200.

1969: Set features rookie card of Reggie Jackson (260) . . . There are two poses each for Clay Dalrymple (151) and Donn Clendenon (208) . . . Aurelio Rodriguez (653) is photo of Lenny Garcia (Angels' bat boy) . . . Card of Mickey Mantle (500) lists for $150 . . . Card of Jackson lists for $175 . . . Complete set lists for $1,200.

1970: Set features rookie cards of Vida Blue (21), Thurman Munson (189) and Bill Buckner (286) . . . Also included are two deceased players Miguel Fuentes (88) and Paul Edmondson (414) who died after cards went to press . . . Card of Johnny Bench (660) lists for $75 . . . Card of Pete Rose (580) lists for $75 . . . Complete set lists for $1,000.

1971: Set features rookie card of Steve Garvey (341) . . . the final series (644-752) is found in lesser quantity and includes rookie card (664) of three pitchers named Reynolds (Archie, Bob and Ken) . . . Card of Garvey lists for $65 . . . Card of Pete Rose (100) lists for $45 . . . Complete set lists for $1,000.

1972: There were 16 cards featuring photos of players in their boyhood years . . . Dave Roberts (91) is photo of Danny Coombs . . . Brewers Rookie Card (162) includes photos of Darrell Porter and Jerry Bell, which were reversed . . . Cards of Steve Garvey (686) and Rod Carew (695) list for $60 . . . Card of Pete Rose (559) lists for $50 . . . Complete set lists for $1,000.

1973: A special Home Run Card (1) depicted Babe Ruth, Hank Aaron and Willie Mays . . . Set features rookie card of Mike Schmidt (615) listing for $175 . . . Joe Rudi (360) is photo of Gene Tenace . . . Card of Pete Rose (130) lists for $18 . . . Card of Reggie Jackson (255) lists for $12.50 . . . Complete set lists for $600.

1974: Set features 15 San Diego Padres cards printed as ''Washington, N.L.'' due to report of franchise move, later corrected . . . Also included was a 44-card Traded Series which updated team changes . . . Set features rookie card of Dave Winfield (456) . . . Card of Mike Schmidt (283) lists for $35 . . . Card of Winfield lists for $25 . . . Complete set lists for $325.

1975: Herb Washington (407) is the only card ever published with position ''designated runner,'' featuring only base-running statistics . . . Set features rookie cards of Robin Yount (223), George Brett (228), Jim Rice (616), Gary Carter (620) and Keith Hernandez (623) . . . Don Wilson (455) died after cards went to press (January 5, 1975) . . . Card of Brett lists for $50 . . . Cards of Rice and Carter list for $35 . . . Complete set lists for $475 . . . TOPPS also tested the complete 660-card series in a smaller size (2¼" x 3 1/8") in certain areas of USA in a limited supply . . . Complete set of ''Mini-Cards'' lists for $700.

1976: As in 1974 there was a 44-card Traded Series . . . Set features five Father & Son cards (66-70) and ten All-Time All-Stars (341-350) . . . Card of Pete Rose (240) lists for $15 . . . Cards of Jim Rice (340), Gary Carter (441) and George Brett (19) list for $12 . . . Complete set lists for $225.

1977: Set features rookie cards of Andre Dawson (473) and Dale Murphy (476) . . . Reuschel Brother Combination (634) shows the two (Paul and Rick) misidentified . . . Dave Collins (431) is photo of Bob Jones . . . Card of Murphy lists for $65 . . . Card of Pete Rose (450) lists for $8.50 . . . Complete set lists for $250.

1978: Record Breakers (1-7) feature Lou Brock, Sparky Lyle, Willie McCovey, Brooks Robinson, Pete Rose, Nolan Ryan and Reggie Jackson . . . Set features rookie cards of Jack Morris (703), Lou Whitaker (704), Paul Molitor/Alan Trammell (707), Lance Parrish (708) and Eddie Murray (36) . . . Card of Murray lists for $35 . . . Card of Parrish lists for $35 . . . Complete set lists for $200.

1979: Bump Wills (369) was originally shown with Blue Jays affiliation but later corrected to Rangers . . . Set features rookie cards of Ozzie Smith (116), Pedro Guerrero (719), Lonnie Smith (722) and Terry Kennedy (724) . . . Larry Cox (489) is photo of Dave Rader . . . Card of Dale Murphy (39) lists for $8 . . . Cards of Ozzie Smith and Eddie Murray (640) list for $7.50 . . . Complete set lists for $135.

1980: Highlights (1-6) feature Hall-of-Famers Lou Brock, Carl Yastrzemski, Willie McCovey and Pete Rose . . . Set features rookie cards of Dave Stieb (77), Rickey Henderson (482) and Dan Quisenberry (667) . . . Card of Henderson lists for $28 . . . Card of Dale Murphy (274) lists for $5.50 . . . Complete set lists for $135.

1981: Set features rookie cards of Fernando Valenzuela (302), Kirk Gibson (315), Harold Baines (347) and Tim Raines (479) . . . Jeff Cox (133) is photo of Steve McCatty . . . John Littlefield (489) is photo of Mark Riggins . . . Card of Valenzuela lists for $7.50 . . . Card of Raines lists for $9 . . . Complete set lists for $80.

1982: Pascual Perez (383) printed with no position on front lists for $35, later corrected . . . Set features rookie cards of Cal Ripken (21), Jesse Barfield (203), Steve Sax (681) and Kent Hrbek (766) . . . Dave Rucker (261) is photo of Roger Weaver . . . Steve Bedrosian (502) is photo of Larry Owen . . . Card of Ripken lists for $12.50 . . . Cards of Barfield and Sax list for $5 . . . Complete set lists for $75.

1983: Record Breakers (1-6) feature Tony Armas, Rickey Henderson, Greg Minton, Lance Parrish, Manny Trillo and John Wathan . . . A series of Super Veterans features early and current photos of 34 leading players . . . Set features rookie cards of Tony Gwynn (482) and Wade Boggs (498) . . . Card of Boggs lists for $32 . . . Card of Gwynn lists for $16 . . . Complete set lists for $85.

1984: Highlights (1-6) salute eleven different players . . . A parade of superstars is included in Active Leaders (701-718) . . . Set features rookie card of Don Mattingly (8) listing for $35 . . . Card of Darryl Strawberry (182) lists for $10 . . . Complete set lists for $85.

1985: A Father & Son Feature (131-143) is again included . . . Set features rookie cards of Scott Bankhead (393), Mike Dunne (395), Shane Mack (398), John Marzano (399), Oddibe McDowell (400), Mark McGwire (401), Pat Pacillo (402), Cory Snyder (403) and Billy Swift (404) as part of salute to 1984 USA Baseball Team (389-404) that participated in Olympic Games plus rookie cards of Roger Clemens (181) and Eric Davis (627) . . . Card of McGwire lists for $20 . . . Card of Davis lists for $18 . . . Card of Clemens lists for $11 . . . Complete set lists for $95.

1986: Set includes Pete Rose Feature (2-7), which reproduces each of Rose's TOPPS cards from 1963 thru 1985 (four per card) . . . Bob Rodgers (141) should have been numbered 171 . . . Ryne Sandberg (690) is the only card with TOPPS logo omitted . . . Complete set lists for $24.

1987: Record Breakers (1-7) feature Roger Clemens, Jim Deshaies, Dwight Evans, Davey Lopes, Dave Righetti, Ruben Sierra and Todd Worrell . . . Jim Gantner (108) is shown with Brewers logo reversed . . . Complete set lists for $22.

1988: Record Breakers (1-7) include Vince Coleman, Don Mattingly, Mark McGwire, Eddie Murray, Phil & Joe Niekro, Nolan Ryan and Benny Santiago. Al Leiter (18) was originally shown with photo of minor leaguer Steve George and later corrected. Complete set lists for $20.00.

Pitching Record & Index

PLAYER	G	IP	W	L	R	ER	SO	BB	GS	CG	SHO	SV	ERA
ABBOTT, GLENN	248	1285	62	83			484	352	206	37	5	0	4.39
ABER, AL	168	390	24	25			169	160	30	7	0	14	4.18
AGUIRRE, HANK	477	1376	75	72			856	479	149	44	9	33	3.24
ALEXANDER, DOYLE	467	2708.1	160	135	1228	1117	1199	803	370	82	13	3	3.71
ANDERSON, BOB	246	841	36	46			502	319	93	15	1	13	4.26
ARROYO, FERNANDO	121	534	24	37			172	157	60	12	2	0	4.45
BAILEY, HOWARD	50	119	6	9			41	40	8	0	0	4	5.22
BAIR, DOUG	443	693.2	47	37			526	313	2	0	0	76	3.54
BAKER, STEVE	84	236.2	7	16			131	127	26	1	0	5	5.13
BARE, RAY	88	340	16	26			145	120	49	9	3	1	4.79
BEARDEN, GENE	193	789	45	38			259	435	84	29	9	1	3.96
BENTON, AL	450	1689	98	88			697	733	167	58	10	66	3.66
BERENGUER, JUAN	183	645	30	41	324	287	498	335	86	5	2	5	4.00
BILLINGHAM, JACK	476	2232	145	113			1141	750	305	74	27	15	3.83
BIRRER, BABE	56	119	4	0			45	37	3	1	0	4	4.39
BOSWELL, DAVE	205	1065	68	56			882	481	151	37	6	0	3.52
BRADY, JIM	6	6	0	0			3	11	0	0	0	0	30.00
BRANCA, RALPH	322	1485	88	68			829	663	188	71	12	19	3.79
BRUCE, BOB	219	1123	49	71			733	340	167	26	6	1	3.85
BUNNING, JIM	591	3759	224	184			2855	1000	519	151	40	16	3.27
BURNSIDE, PETE	196	569	19	36			203	230	64	14	3	7	4.79
BYRD, HARRY	187	827	46	54			381	355	108	33	8	9	4.35
CAIN, BOB	140	629	37	44			249	316	89	27	8	8	4.49
CAIN, LES	68	374	19	19			303	225	64	8	1	0	3.97
CAMPBELL, BILL	693	1219.2	83	68	538	475	860	491	9	2	1	126	3.51
CAPPUZZELLO, GEORGE	35	53.1	1	2			32	25	3	0	0	0	3.21
CARY, CHUCK	38	55.1	1	0	27	21	43	23	0	0	0	0	3.42
CASALE, JERRY	96	371	17	24			207	204	49	10	3	1	5.07
CHANCE, DEAN	406	2148	128	115			1534	739	294	83	33	23	2.92
CHRIS, MIKE	29	78.1	3	5			46	63	14	0	0	0	6.43
CICOTTE, AL	102	260	10	13			149	119	16	0	0	4	4.36
COLEMAN, JOE H.	484	2571	142	135			1728	1003	340	94	18	6	3.69
COLEMAN, JOE P.	223	1133	52	76			444	566	140	60	11	0	4.38
CONNELLY, BILL	25	66	6	2			34	53	7	1	0	0	6.95
CRAWFORD, JIM	181	431	15	28			276	182	14	1	0	13	4.41
CRIMIAN, JACK	74	160	5	9			69	65	7	0	0	4	6.35
DAVIE, JERRY	11	37	2	2			20	17	5	1	0	0	4.14
DENEHY, BILL	49	105	1	10			63	61	7	0	0	2	4.54
DOBSON, PAT	414	2119	122	129			1301	665	279	74	14	19	3.54
DONOHUE, JIM	71	262	12	16			116	82	33	3	0	7	4.27
DONOVAN, DICK	345	2020	122	99			880	495	273	101	25	5	3.66
DUSTAL, BOB	7	5	0	1			4	5	0	0	0	0	9.00
EGAN, DICK	74	101	0	1			68	41	0	0	0	2	5.17
FACE, ROY	848	1375	104	95			877	362	27	6	0	193	3.48
FARMER, ED	370	624	30	43			395	345	21	1	0	75	4.30
FAUL, BILL	71	262	12	16			164	95	33	8	3	0	4.71
FIDRYCH, MARK	58	412	29	19			170	99	56	34	5	0	3.10
FISCHER, BILL	281	832	45	58			313	210	78	16	2	13	4.34
FISHER, FRITZ	1	2	0	0					0	0	0	0	108.0
FOOR, JIM	13	6	0	0			5	11	0	0	0	0	12.00
FOUCAULT, STEVE	277	496	35	36			307	190	0	0	0	52	3.21
FOX, TERRY	248	396	29	19			185	124	0	0	0	59	3.00
FOYTACK, PAUL	312	1499	86	87			827	662	193	63	7	7	4.14
FRYMAN, WOODIE	625	2411.2	141	155			1587	890	322	68	27	58	3.77

PLAYER	G	IP	W	L	R	ER	SO	BB	GS	CG	SHO	SV	ERA
GLADDING, FRED	450	600	48	34			394	223	1	0	0	109	3.13
GLYNN, ED	172	263	12	17			181	147	8	1	0	12	4.11
GRAY, TED	222	1133	59	74			687	595	162	50	7	4	4.37
GRILLI, STEVE	70	148	4	3			91	96	2	0	0	4	4.50
GRISSOM, MARV	356	810	47	45			459	343	52	12	3	58	3.41
GROMEK, STEVE	447	2065	123	108			904	630	225	92	15	23	3.41
GRZENDA, JOE	219	309	14	13			173	120	3	0	0	14	3.99
GUMPERT, DAVE	78	116.1	3	3	61	52	63	44	1	0	0	5	4.02
HAMILTON, JACK	218	612	32	40			357	238	65	8	2	20	4.53
HANNAN, JIM	276	822	41	48			438	406	101	9	2	7	3.88
HARRIST, EARL	132	383	12	28			162	193	24	5	1	10	4.34
HERBERT, RAY	407	1883	104	107			864	571	236	68	13	15	4.01
HERNANDEZ, WILLIE	604	897	59	52	359	329	669	282	11	0	0	114	3.30
HILLER, JOHN	545	1241	87	76			1036	535	43	13	6	125	2.84
HOEFT, BILLY	505	1848	97	101			1140	685	200	75	17	33	3.94
HOLDSWORTH, FRED	72	183	7	10			94	86	15	0	0	2	4.38
HOUTTEMAN, ART	325	1556	87	91			639	516	181	78	14	20	4.14
HUMPHREYS, BOB	319	568	27	21			364	219	4	0	0	20	3.34
HUTCHINSON, FREDDY	242	1465	95	71			591	388	169	81	13	7	3.72
JAMES, BOB	236	353	20	20	162	144	306	140	2	0	0	63	3.67
JONES, SAM	322	1644	102	101			1376	822	222	76	17	9	3.59
KILKENNY, MIKE	139	409	23	18			301	224	54	12	4	3	4.44
KING, ERIC	33	138.1	11	4	54	54	79	63	16	3	1	3	3.51
KINNEY, DENNIS	97	155.1	4	9			75	71	0	0	0	6	4.52
KLINE, RON	736	2078	114	144			989	731	203	44	6	108	3.86
KLIPPSTEIN, JOHNNY	711	1970	101	118			1158	978	162	37	6	66	4.24
KOPLITZ, HOWIE	54	176	9	7			87	80	19	2	0	1	4.19
KORINCE, GEORGE	11	17	1	0			13	14	0	0	0	0	4.24
KRETLOW, LOU	199	786	27	47			450	522	104	22	3	1	4.87
LABINE, CLEM	513	1080	77	56			551	396	38	7	2	96	3.63
LAGROW, LERRIN	309	778	34	55			375	312	67	19	2	54	4.12
LAPOINT, DAVE	191	898.2	46	49	453	396	532	358	131	5	2	1	3.97
LARY, FRANK	350	2162	128	116			1099	616	292	126	21	11	3.49
LASHER, FRED	151	202	11	13			148	110	1	0	0	22	3.88
LAXTON, BILL	121	244	3	10			189	158	4	0	0	5	4.72
LAZORKO, JACK	15	39.2	0	1			24	22	4	0	0	1	4.31
LEE, DON	244	828	40	44			467	281	97	13	4	11	3.61
LEMANCZYK, DAVE	185	912	37	63	370	341	429	363	103	30	3	1	4.63
LITTLEFIELD, DICK	243	761	33	54			495	413	83	16	2	9	4.72
LOLICH, MICKEY	586	3640	217	191			2832	1099	496	195	41	11	3.44
LOPEZ, AURELIO	433	872.1	60	35	242	211	614	355	91	7	1	92	3.52
MAAS, DUKE	195	734	45	44			356	284	91	21	7	15	4.19
MADISON, DAVE	74	158	8	7			70	103	6	0	0	4	5.70
MAHLER, MICKEY	122	406	14	32	59	50	262	190	58	3	1	4	4.68
MARSHALL, MIKE G.	723	1386	97	112			880	514	24	3	1	187	3.15
MARTIN, JOHN	91	290.2	17	14			120	95	32	2	1	1	3.93
MASON, ROGER	21	111.2	5	8			84	51	18	2	1	1	4.03
MASTERSON, WALT	399	1648	78	100			815	886	184	70	15	20	4.15
McDERMOTT, MICKEY	291	1316	69	69			757	838	156	54	11	14	3.91
McLAIN, DENNY	280	1809	131	91			1282	548	264	105	29	2	3.54
McMAHON, DON	874	1312	90	68			1003	579	2	0	0	153	2.96
McRAE, NORM	22	34	0	0			19	26	0	0	0	0	3.18
MILLER, BOB G.	86	189	6	8			75	92	8	1	0	1	4.71
MILLER, BOB L.	694	1552	69	81			895	608	99	7	0	52	3.37
MOFORD, HERB	50	158	3	13			78	64	14	6	0	3	5.01

PLAYER	G	IP	W	L	R	ER	SO	BB	GS	CG	SHO	SV	ERA
MONGE, SID	435	764.1	49	40			471	356	17	4	0	56	3.53
MORGAN, TOM	443	1025	67	47			364	300	61	18	0	64	3.60
MORRIS, JACK	302	2122.1	144	94	910	842	1327	754	280	110	19	0	3.57
MOSSI, DON	460	1548	101	80			932	385	165	55	8	50	3.43
NARLESKI, RAY	266	701	43	33			454	335	52	17	1	58	3.61
NAVARRO, JULIO	130	211	7	9			151	70	1	0	0	17	3.67
NEWHOUSER, HAL	488	2993	207	150			1796	1249	374	212	33	26	3.05
NEWSOM, BOBO	600	3758	211	222			2082	1732	483	246	30	21	3.99
NIEKRO, JOE	670	3426	213	190	1506	1331	1656	1191	472	106	29	16	3.50
NISCHWITZ, RON	88	116	5	8			58	48	1	0	0	6	3.50
NOLES, DICKIE	229	789.2	32	48	447	400	421	310	93	3	0	7	4.19
O'NEAL, RANDY	69	235.2	10	3	118	100	132	86	26	2	0	3	4.56
OVERMIRE, FRANK	266	1130	58	67			301	325	137	50	11	3	3.82
PACELLA, JOHN	69	180.1	4	10			111	120	21	0	0	2	3.97
PATTERSON, DARYL	142	231	11	9			142	119	3	0	0	11	5.84
PENA, ORLANDO	427	1203	56	77			818	352	93	21	4	40	4.09
PENTZ, GENE	104	191	8	9			116	108	4	0	0	6	3.70
PERRANOSKI, RON	737	1176	79	74			687	468	1	0	0	179	3.63
PERRY, JIM	630	3287	215	174			1580	998	447	109	32	10	2.79
PETRY, DAN	227	1504.1	98	74	675	599	773	572	224	47	10	0	3.44
PIERCE, BILLY	585	3305	211	169			1999	1178	432	193	38	32	3.58
PODRES, JOHNNY	440	2265	148	116			1435	743	340	77	24	11	3.67
PRESKO, JOE	128	492	25	37			202	188	61	15	0	5	4.59
PROCTOR, JIM	2	3	0	1			0	1	0	0	0	0	15.00
RADATZ, DICK	381	694	52	43			745	296	0	0	0	122	3.13
RAKOW, ED	195	760	36	47			484	304	90	20	3	5	4.33
RAY, JIM	308	618	45	30			407	271	21	1	0	25	3.61
REED, BOB	24	61	2	4			35	22	5	0	0	2	4.13
REGAN, PHIL	551	1373	96	81			743	447	105	20	1	92	3.83
REYNOLDS, BOB	140	254	14	16			167	82	2	0	0	21	3.15
RIBANT, DENNIS	149	519	24	29			241	126	56	12	2	0	3.87
ROBBINS, BRUCE A.	25	49	7	5			45	49	14	0	0	0	5.33
ROBERTS, DAVE A.	445	2098	103	125			957	615	277	77	20	15	3.78
ROBERTSON, JERRY	49	195	5	16			144	86	27	3	0	2	3.92
ROGOVIN, SAUL	150	885	48	48			388	308	121	43	9	2	4.06
ROOKER, JIM	319	1811	103	109			976	703	255	66	15	7	3.46
ROWE, SCHOOLBOY	382	2219	158	101			913	558	278	137	22	12	3.87
ROZEMA, DAVE	242	1094.2	60	53			445	255	132	36	7	17	3.44
RUCKER, DAVE	156	266.1	16	16			140	124	10	1	0	11	3.68
RUHLE, VERN	327	1410.2	67	88			582	348	188	29	12	11	3.73
SAUCIER, KEVIN	139	203.1	15	11			94	104	3	0	0	19	3.32
SAUNDERS, DENNIS	8	14	1	1			8	5	0	0	0	0	3.21
SCARBOROUGH, RAY	318	1429	80	85			564	611	168	59	8	14	4.13
SCHATZEDER, DAN	328	1077	58	59			378	378	118	18	4	6	3.58
SCHERMAN, FRED	346	537	33	26			297	245	8	0	0	39	3.84
SCHERRER, BILL	193	267.2	7	8			177	119	2	0	0	11	3.87
SCHULTZ, BARNEY	227	347	20	20			264	116	19	3	0	35	3.63
SCHULTZ, BOB	65	182	9	13			67	125	19	3	0	5	5.19
SEELBACH, CHUCK	85	131	10	8			79	51	3	0	0	14	3.37
SEMPROCH, RAY	85	344	19	21			156	136	48	14	2	3	4.42
SHAW, BOB	430	1779	108	98			880	511	223	55	15	32	3.52
SISLER, DAVE	247	655	38	44			355	368	59	12	1	29	4.34
SLATON, JIM	496	2683.2	151	158	1335	1202	1191	1004	360	86	22	14	4.03
SLAYBACK, BILL	42	139	6	9			89	51	17	3	1	0	3.82
SLEATER, LOU	131	301	12	18			152	172	21	7	1	5	4.69
SMITH, BOB G.	91	167	4	9			93	83	8	2	0	2	4.04
SNELL, NATE	82	180.1	6	4			71	53	0	0	0	5	3.14
SOSA, ELIAS	601	919.1	59	51			538	334	3	0	0	83	3.32
SPARMA, JOE	183	865	52	52			586	436	142	31	10	0	3.94
SPENCER, GEORGE	122	251	16	10			82	106	9	3	0	9	4.05
STALEY, GERRY	640	1981	134	111			727	529	186	58	9	61	3.70

No major league statistics

PLAYER	G	IP	W	L	R	ER	SO	BB	GS	CG	SHO	SV	ERA
STODDARD, BOB	76	357	16	24			172	122	43	5	2	0	4.01
STRAHLER, MIKE	53	159	6	8			80	79	13	2	0	1	3.57
STRAMPE, BOB	7	5	0	0			4	7	0	0	0	0	3.57
STUART, MARLIN	196	486	23	17			185	256	31	7	0	15	4.65
STURDIVANT, TOM	335	1136	59	51			704	449	101	22	7	17	3.75
SUSCE, GEORGE	117	410	22	17			177	170	36	8	1	3	4.41
SYKES, BOB	116	457	23	26			215	190	61	3	0	2	4.65
TANANA, FRANK	408	2758.1	159	153	1180	1041	1925	772	392	123	28	2	3.40
TAYLOR, BRUCE	30	49	3	2			27	17	0	0	0	2	3.86
TERRELL, WALT	125	816	49	45	391	353	404	342	123	21	8	0	3.89
THURMOND, MARK	131	554.2	35	30	251	216	212	176	89	6	3	5	3.50
TIMMERMANN, TOM	228	548	35	35			315	208	44	8	2	35	3.78
TOBIK, DAVE	188	387	21	23			248	150	2	0	0	27	3.65
TROUT, DIZZY	521	2726	170	161			1256	1046	322	158	28	35	3.23
TRUCKS, VIRGIL	517	2684	177	135			1534	1088	328	124	33	30	3.38
TSITOURIS, JOHN	149	662	34	38			432	260	84	18	5	3	4.13
UJDUR, JERRY	53	261.1	12	16			118	110	40	7	0	0	4.79
UNDERWOOD, PAT	113	344.1	13	18			188	92	34	3	0	8	4.42
VALENTINETTI, VITO	108	257	13	14			94	122	15	3	0	3	4.73
WALKER, LUKE	279	941	48	55			618	448	109	17	7	9	3.74
WALKER, TOM	191	415	18	23			262	142	17	2	0	11	3.86
WARDEN, JON	28	37	4	1			25	15	0	0	0	3	3.65
WEAVER, ROGER	19	64	3	4			42	34	6	0	0	0	4.08
WEHMEIER, HERMAN	361	1804	92	108			794	852	240	79	9	9	4.79
WEIK, DICK	76	213	6	22			123	237	26	3	2	1	5.92
WICKERSHAM, DAVE	228	1123	68	57			638	384	124	29	5	18	3.66
WIGHT, BILL	347	1562	77	99			574	714	198	66	15	8	3.95
WILCOX, MILT	381	1958.1	119	105			1111	742	273	73	10	6	4.04
WILLIS, CARL	57	91.2	2	6			37	44	2	0	0	2	5.60
WILSON, EARL	338	2052	121	109			1452	796	310	69	13	0	3.69
WOODESHICK, HAL	427	847	44	62			484	389	62	7	1	61	3.56
WYATT, JOHN	435	686	42	44			540	346	9	0	0	103	3.48
WYATT, WHITLOW	360	1762	106	95			872	642	210	97	17	13	3.78
YOUNG, KIP	27	150	8	9			71	41	20	7	1	0	3.84
ZACHARY, CHRIS	108	321	10	29			184	122	40	1	1	2	4.51
ZEPP, BILL	63	188	10	5			81	72	24	1	1	4	3.64
ZUVERINK, GEORGE	265	642	32	36			223	203	31	9	2	40	3.54

Batting Record & Index

PLAYER	G	AB	R	H	2B	3B	HR	RBI	SB	SLG	BB	SO	AVG
ALUSIK, GEORGE	298	657	75	167	31	2	23	93	1	.416	73	103	.256
ALVARADO, LUIS	463	1160	116	248	43	4	5	84	11	.271	47	160	.214
ALVAREZ, OSSIE	95	198	20	42	3	0	0	5	1	.227	16	27	.212
AMOROS, SANDY	517	1311	215	334	55	23	43	180	18	.430	211	189	.255
ANDERSON, SPARKY	152	477	42	104	9	3	0	34	6	.249	42	53	.218
APPLING, LUKE	2422	8857	1319	2749	440	102	45	1116	179	.398	1302	528	.310
BAKER, DEL	172	302	27	63	9	4	0	22	0	.265	32	32	.209
BAKER, DOUG	43	108	15	20	4	1	0	11	3	.241	7	22	.185
BATTS, MATT	546	1605	163	432	95	11	26	219	6	.391	143	163	.269
BERBERET, LOU	448	1224	118	281	34	10	31	153	2	.350	200	195	.230
BERGMAN, DAVE	732	1253	151	301	43	10	26	130	13	.360	179	170	.240
BERTOIA, RENO	612	1745	204	425	60	10	27	171	16	.336	142	252	.244
BILKO, STEVE	600	1738	220	432	85	13	76	276	1	.444	234	395	.249
BOLLING, FRANK	1540	5562	692	1415	221	40	106	556	40	.366	462	558	.254
BOLLING, MILT	400	1161	127	280	50	7	19	94	5	.345	115	188	.241
BOONE, RAY	1373	4589	645	1260	162	46	151	737	21	.429	608	463	.275
BOROS, STEVE	422	1255	141	308	50	7	26	149	11	.359	181	174	.245
BRIDEWESER, JIM	329	620	79	156	22	6	1	50	6	.310	63	78	.252
BRIDGES, ROCKY	919	2272	245	562	80	11	16	187	10	.313	205	229	.247
BRINKMAN, ED	1845	6045	552	1355	201	38	59	461	30	.299	444	845	.224
BROOKENS, TOM	927	2658	324	657	124	30	48	300	74	.371	179	416	.247
BROWN, DARRELL	210	591	82	157	15	6	1	44	9	.325	25	47	.274
BROWN, DICK	636	1866	175	475	72	6	62	223	7	.380	117	356	.244
BROWN, GATES	1051	2262	330	582	78	19	84	322	33	.420	242	275	.257
BROWN, IKE	280	536	85	137	15	4	20	65	3	.410	90	130	.256
BRUTON, BILL	1610	6056	937	1651	241	102	94	545	207	.393	482	793	.273
BUCHA, JOHNNY	84	195	18	40	10	0	1	15	0	.272	25	21	.205
BUDDIN, DON	711	2289	342	551	123	12	41	225	15	.359	410	404	.241
BUTERA, SAL	280	619	52	147	17	2	5	56	0	.296	77	54	.237
CABELL, ENOS	1688	5952	753	1647	263	56	60	596	238	.370	259	691	.277
CAMPBELL, DAVE	428	1252	128	267	54	4	20	89	43	.311	102	254	.213
CASH, NORM	2089	6705	1046	1820	241	41	377	1103	43	.488	1043	1091	.271
CASH, RON	34	101	14	30	3	1	2	11	0	.347	5	16	.297
CASTILLO, MARTY	201	352	31	67	13	1	8	32	3	.301	19	76	.190
CHITI, HARRY	502	1495	135	356	49	9	41	179	4	.365	115	242	.238
CHRISLEY, NEIL	302	619	60	130	22	8	16	64	3	.349	55	62	.210
CHRISTIAN, BOB	54	147	13	33	5	0	4	19	3	.340	11	23	.224
COBB, TY	3034	11437	2245	4191	724	297	118	1933	892	.513	1249	357	.367
COCHRANE, MICKEY	1482	5169	1041	1652	333	64	119	832	64	.478	857	217	.320
COLAVITO, ROCKY	1841	6503	971	1730	283	21	374	1159	19	.489	951	880	.266
COLBERT, NATE	1004	3422	481	833	141	25	173	520	52	.451	383	902	.243
COLES, DARNELL	244	815	99	205	44	3	32	103	8	.394	78	139	.251
COLLINS, DAVE	1368	4484	612	1231	171	50	32	344	369	.356	422	594	.275
COLLINS, KEVIN	201	388	30	81	17	4	6	34	1	.320	20	97	.209
COMER, WAYNE	316	687	119	157	22	4	16	67	22	.336	106	102	.229
CORCORAN, TIM	503	1043	119	283	46	4	12	128	4	.358	128	106	.271
COTTIER, CHUCK	580	1584	168	348	63	17	19	127	28	.317	137	248	.220
COWENS, AL	1556	5452	699	1479	272	68	108	711	119	.406	386	641	.271
DELSING, JIM	822	2461	322	627	112	21	40	286	15	.366	299	251	.255
DEMETER, DON	1109	3443	467	912	147	17	163	563	22	.459	180	658	.265
DIDIER, BOB	247	751	56	172	25	4	1	51	0	.273	59	72	.229
DILLARD, STEVE	438	1013	148	246	50	6	13	102	15	.343	76	147	.243
DITTMER, JACK	395	1218	117	283	43	4	24	136	4	.333	77	102	.232
DOBY, LARRY	1533	5348	960	1515	243	52	253	969	47	.490	871	1011	.283
DRESSEN, CHUCK	646	2215	313	603	123	29	11	221	30	.385	219	118	.272

PLAYER	G	AB	R	H	2B	3B	HR	RBI	SB	SLG	BB	SO	AVG
DYER, DUFFY	722	1993	151	441	74	11	30	173	10	.315	228	415	.221
DYKES, JIMMY	2282	8046	1108	2256	453	90	109	1071	70	.400	954	849	.280
ENGLE, DAVE	439	1371	179	368	71	13	28	154	4	.400	98	148	.268
EVANS, DARRELL	2286	7761	1175	1947	294	35	347	1152	91	.432	1380	1191	.251
EVERS, HOOT	1142	3801	556	1055	187	41	98	565	45	.426	415	420	.278
FAHEY, BILL	383	934	75	225	26	2	7	83	9	.296	74	93	.241
FAIN, FERRIS	1151	3930	595	1139	213	30	48	570	46	.396	903	261	.290
FARLEY, BOB	84	123	19	20	3	1	2	9	0	.252	28	28	.163
FERNANDEZ, CHICO	856	2778	270	666	91	19	40	259	68	.329	213	338	.240
FINIGAN, JIM	512	1600	195	422	74	17	19	168	8	.367	190	176	.264
FLYNN, DOUG	1308	3853	179	918	115	39	7	284	20	.294	151	320	.238
FOILES, HANK	608	1455	171	353	59	10	46	166	3	.392	170	295	.243
FRANCONA, TITO	1719	5121	650	1395	224	34	125	656	46	.403	544	694	.272
FREEHAN, BILL	1774	6073	706	1591	241	35	200	758	24	.412	626	420	.262
FRIEND, OWEN	208	598	69	136	24	2	13	76	2	.339	55	109	.227
FUENTES, TITO	1499	5566	610	1491	211	46	45	438	80	.347	298	561	.268
GAMBLE, JOHN	13	3	1	0	0	0	0	0	0	.000	0	0	.000
GARBEY, BARBARO	196	564	72	155	26	2	11	81	9	.387	32	72	.275
GARCIA, PEDRO	558	1797	196	395	89	15	37	184	35	.348	102	329	.220
GERNERT, DICK	835	2493	357	632	104	8	103	402	10	.426	363	462	.254
GIBSON, KIRK	765	2723	433	750	115	32	126	420	140	.480	309	596	.275
GINSBERG, JOE	695	1716	168	414	59	4	20	182	7	.320	226	135	.241
GOLDY, PURNAL	29	78	9	18	1	1	3	12	0	.385	3	16	.231
GONZALEZ, JULIO	370	969	90	228	32	8	4	66	13	.297	36	132	.235
GORDON, JOE	1566	5707	914	1530	264	52	253	975	89	.466	759	702	.268
GREEN, LENNY	1136	3056	461	788	138	27	47	253	88	.379	260	260	.267
GREENE, AL	29	59	9	8	1	0	3	6	1	.305	10	15	.136
GROTH, JOHNNY	1248	3808	480	1064	197	29	60	486	19	.395	411	329	.279
GRUBB, JOHNNY	1365	4040	544	1130	201	29	97	462	27	.416	551	542	.280
GUTIERREZ, CESAR	223	545	61	128	13	6	0	26	7	.281	30	51	.235
HALLER, TOM	1294	3935	461	1011	153	21	134	504	14	.414	477	593	.257
HANEY, FRED	622	1977	338	544	66	21	8	228	50	.342	282	123	.275
HARPER, BRIAN	175	337	30	82	13	1	11	44	1	.386	10	34	.243
HARPER, TERRY	473	1337	135	339	49	5	32	163	36	.369	135	229	.254
HARRIS, GAIL	437	1331	159	320	38	15	51	190	2	.406	106	194	.240
HATFIELD, FRED	722	2039	259	493	67	10	25	165	15	.321	248	247	.242
HAZLE, BOB	110	261	37	81	14	1	9	37	1	.467	32	35	.310
HEATH, BILL	112	199	13	47	6	1	0	13	1	.276	26	22	.236
HEATH, MIKE	853	2818	316	698	113	20	55	325	38	.361	189	375	.248
HEBNER, RICH	1908	6144	865	1694	273	57	203	890	38	.438	687	741	.276
HEFFNER, DON	743	2526	275	610	99	19	6	248	18	.303	270	248	.241
HEGAN, JIM	1666	4772	550	1087	187	46	92	525	15	.344	456	742	.228
HERNDON, LARRY	1372	4478	557	1222	168	74	94	483	91	.406	307	721	.273
HERZOG, WHITEY	634	1614	213	414	60	20	25	172	13	.365	241	261	.257
HIGGINS, MIKE	1802	6636	930	1941	374	50	141	1075	61	.428	800	590	.292
HITCHCOCK, BILLY	703	2249	257	547	67	22	5	257	22	.299	205	230	.243
HOPP, JOHNNY	1393	4260	698	1262	216	74	46	458	128	.414	465	358	.296
HORTON, WILLIE	2028	7298	873	1993	284	40	325	1163	20	.457	620	1313	.273
HOSLEY, TIM	208	368	43	79	11	0	12	53	0	.342	57	73	.215
HOUK, RALPH	91	158	12	43	9	1	0	20	0	.323	12	10	.272
HOUSE, FRANK	653	1994	202	494	64	11	47	235	8	.362	151	147	.248
HOWARD, FRANK	1895	6488	864	1774	245	35	382	1119	8	.499	782	1460	.273
HUMPHREY, TERRY	415	1055	69	223	39	1	6	85	5	.267	68	175	.211
IVIE, MIKE	857	2694	309	724	133	17	81	411	22	.421	214	402	.269
JACKSON, RON	926	2986	356	774	165	22	56	342	18	.385	213	329	.259

PLAYER	G	AB	R	H	2B	3B	HR	RBI	SB	SLG	BB	SO	AVG
JATA, PAUL	32	74	8	17	2	0	0	3	0	.257	7	14	.230
JOHNSON, ALEX	1322	4623	550	1331	180	33	78	525	103	.392	244	626	.288
JOHNSON, HOWARD	411	1185	145	299	51	5	40	154	31	.405	128	249	.252
JONES, DALTON	907	2329	268	548	91	19	41	237	20	.343	191	309	.235
JONES, LYNN	460	900	108	233	32	5	7	90	13	.329	67	80	.259
JONES, RUPPERT	1246	4223	618	1056	207	36	139	551	141	.415	514	779	.250
KALINE, AL	2834	10116	1622	3007	498	75	399	1583	137	.480	1277	1020	.297
KELL, GEORGE	1795	6702	881	2054	385	50	78	870	51	.414	620	287	.306
KELLEHER, MICK	622	1081	108	230	32	6	0	65	9	.253	74	133	.213
KEMP, STEVE	1139	4006	578	1117	179	25	129	631	37	.433	570	590	.279
KENNEDY, BOB	1483	4624	514	1176	196	41	63	514	45	.355	364	443	.254
KIMM, BRUCE	186	439	35	104	19	1	1	26	5	.292	32	50	.237
KING, CHICK	45	76	11	18	0	1	0	5	0	.263	8	18	.237
KNOX, JOHN	124	219	21	60	4	1	0	11	7	.301	20	27	.274
KOLLOWAY, DON	1079	3993	466	1081	180	30	29	393	76	.353	189	251	.271
KOSTRO, FRANK	266	467	40	114	17	2	5	37	0	.321	33	85	.244
KRENCHICKI, WAYNE	550	1063	107	283	44	5	15	124	7	.359	106	141	.266
KRESS, CHARLIE	175	466	57	116	20	7	1	52	6	.328	49	59	.249
KRESS, RED	1391	5087	691	1454	298	58	89	799	47	.420	474	453	.286
KRYHOSKI, DICK	569	1794	203	475	85	14	45	231	5	.403	119	163	.265
KUENN, HARVEY	1833	6913	951	2092	356	56	87	671	68	.408	594	404	.303
KUNTZ, RUSTY	272	436	75	104	23	0	5	38	5	.326	58	104	.239
LAGA, MIKE	90	247	25	58	15	0	11	36	1	.429	16	74	.235
LAMONT, GENE	87	159	15	37	8	1	4	14	1	.371	9	35	.233
LANDIS, JIM	1346	4288	625	1061	169	50	93	467	139	.375	588	767	.247
LAU, CHARLIE	527	1170	105	298	63	9	16	140	3	.365	109	150	.255
LEACH, RICK	426	912	102	234	47	7	12	96	6	.363	80	112	.257
LEFLORE, RON	1099	4458	731	1283	172	57	59	353	455	.446	363	888	.288
LEMON, CHET	1467	5150	747	1429	302	48	166	666	53	.451	526	745	.277
LENHARDT, DON	481	1481	192	401	64	9	61	239	6	.450	214	235	.271
LEPCIO, TED	729	2092	233	512	91	11	69	251	11	.398	210	471	.245
LIPON, JOHNNY	758	2661	351	690	95	24	10	266	28	.324	347	152	.259
LOWRY, DWIGHT	88	195	29	57	6	0	5	25	0	.400	20	30	.292
LUMPE, JERRY	1371	4912	620	1314	190	52	47	454	20	.356	428	411	.268
LUND, DON	281	753	91	181	36	8	15	86	5	.369	65	113	.240
MADDOX, ELLIOTT	1029	2843	360	742	121	16	18	234	60	.334	409	358	.261
MADLOCK, BILL	1698	6207	859	1906	330	34	146	803	170	.442	571	460	.307
MANKOWSKI, PHIL	269	739	72	195	23	4	8	64	3	.338	55	103	.264
MANUEL, JERRY	96	127	14	19	6	1	3	12	0	.283	10	26	.150
MANUSH, HEINIE	2009	7653	1287	2524	491	160	110	1173	114	.479	506	354	.330
MAPES, CLIFF	459	1193	199	289	55	13	38	172	8	.406	168	213	.242
MARTIN, BILLY	1021	3419	425	877	137	28	64	333	34	.369	187	355	.257
MARTING, TIM	No major league statistics												
MATCHICK, TOM	292	826	63	178	21	6	4	64	6	.270	39	148	.215
MATHEWS, EDDIE	2391	8537	1509	2315	354	72	512	1453	68	.509	1444	1487	.271
MAXWELL, CHARLIE	1133	3245	478	856	110	26	148	532	18	.451	484	545	.264
MAY, MILT	1192	3693	313	971	147	11	77	443	4	.371	305	361	.265
MAYO, EDDIE	834	3013	350	759	119	16	26	287	29	.328	258	175	.252
MCAULIFFE, DICK	1763	6185	888	1530	231	71	197	697	63	.403	882	974	.247
MCCOSKY, BARNEY	1170	4172	664	1301	214	71	24	397	58	.414	497	261	.312
MCFARLANE, ORLANDO	124	292	22	70	12	0	5	20	0	.332	20	93	.240
MELVIN, BOB	130	350	34	78	18	3	5	29	3	.334	18	90	.223
METRO, CHARLIE	171	358	42	69	10	2	3	23	3	.257	36	55	.193
MEYER, DAN	1104	3722	409	944	153	31	86	459	61	.381	218	297	.254
MICHAEL, GENE	973	2806	249	642	86	12	15	226	22	.284	234	421	.229
MILLER, ED	138	332	63	79	6	2	1	17	49	.277	19	71	.238
MOLINARO, BOB	401	803	106	212	25	11	14	90	45	.375	65	57	.264
MOORE, JACKIE	21	53	2	5	0	0	0	2	0	.094	6	12	.094
MORALES, JERRY	1441	4528	516	1173	199	36	95	570	37	.382	366	567	.259
MORRISON, JIM	884	2744	302	730	140	14	97	351	40	.433	174	411	.266
MORTON, BUBBA	451	928	117	248	37	8	14	128	7	.370	111	143	.267

PLAYER	G	AB	R	H	2B	3B	HR	RBI	SB	SLG	BB	SO	AVG
MOSES, GERRY	385	1072	89	269	48	8	25	109	1	.381	63	184	.251
MULLIN, PAT	864	2493	381	676	106	43	87	385	20	.453	330	312	.271
NAGELSON, RUSS	62	76	9	16	1	0	1	4	0	.263	13	20	.211
NAHORODNY, BILL	308	844	74	203	41	3	25	109	1	.385	56	118	.241
NETTLES, JIM	240	587	68	129	15	4	16	57	10	.341	70	109	.220
NIEMAN, BOB	1113	3452	455	1018	180	32	125	544	10	.474	435	512	.295
NORMAN, BILL	37	103	13	21	5	1	0	8	0	.272	6	13	.204
NORTHRUP, JIM	1392	4692	603	1254	218	42	153	610	39	.429	449	635	.267
O'NEILL, STEVE	1586	4795	448	1259	248	34	13	537	30	.337	592	283	.263
OGLIVIE, BEN	1754	5913	784	1615	277	33	235	901	87	.450	560	852	.273
OLSON, KARL	279	681	74	160	25	6	6	50	3	.316	43	94	.235
OSBORNE, LARRY	359	763	93	157	30	2	17	86	2	.317	104	171	.206
OYLER, RAY	542	1265	110	221	39	6	15	86	2	.251	135	359	.175
PAPI, STAN	225	523	49	114	26	6	7	51	2	.331	24	99	.278
PARKER, SALTY	11	25	6	7	2	0	0	4	0	.360	2	3	.280
PARRISH, LANCE	1146	4273	577	1123	201	23	212	700	22	.469	335	847	.263
PESKY, JOHNNY	1270	4745	867	1455	226	50	17	404	53	.386	663	218	.307
PETERS, RICK	263	881	128	248	33	10	2	79	18	.348	100	100	.281
PHILLEY, DAVE	1904	6296	789	1700	276	72	84	729	102	.377	596	551	.270
PHILLIPS, BUBBA	1062	3278	348	835	135	8	62	356	25	.358	182	314	.255
PHILLIPS, JACK	343	892	111	252	42	16	9	101	5	.396	85	86	.283
PIERCE, JACK	7O	199	20	42	6	1	8	22	0	.372	22	48	.211
PITTARO, CHRIS	27	62	10	15	3	0	1	7	1	.323	5	13	.242
PORTER, J.W.	229	544	58	124	22	1	8	62	4	.316	53	96	.228
PRICE, JIMMIE	261	602	58	129	22	0	18	71	0	.341	62	70	.214
PRIDDY, GERRY	1296	4720	612	1252	232	46	61	541	44	.373	624	639	.265
PUTMAN, EDDY	43	71	6	17	3	0	2	7	0	.366	8	18	.239
REDMOND, WAYNE	9	7	1	0	0	0	0	0	0	.000	1	3	.000
REESE, RICH	866	2020	248	512	73	17	52	245	16	.384	158	270	.253
RICHARDS, PAUL	523	1417	140	321	51	5	15	155	15	.301	157	149	.227
ROARKE, MIKE	194	491	41	113	11	2	6	44	0	.297	45	61	.230
ROBERTS, LEON	901	2737	342	731	126	28	78	328	26	.419	256	428	.267
ROBINSON, EDDIE	1314	4279	545	1145	171	24	172	723	10	.439	520	359	.268
RODRIGUEZ, AURELIO	2017	6611	612	1570	287	46	124	648	35	.351	324	943	.237
ROLFE, RED	1175	4827	942	1394	257	67	69	497	44	.413	526	335	.289
ROMAN, BILL	24	35	2	5	0	0	1	1	0	.229	2	9	.143
SAMFORD, RON	158	334	31	73	14	2	5	27	2	.317	17	46	.219
SANCHEZ, ALEJANDRO	99	195	27	47	7	3	8	20	4	.431	0	57	.241
SANDERS, REGGIE	26	99	12	27	7	0	3	10	1	.434	5	20	.273
SCHEFFING, BOB	517	1357	105	357	53	9	20	187	6	.360	103	127	.263
SCHULTZ, JOE	240	328	18	85	13	1	1	46	0	.314	37	21	.259
SCRIVENER, CHUCK	145	310	38	59	8	1	2	18	2	.242	24	44	.190
SHARON, DICK	242	467	46	102	20	0	13	46	6	.345	50	95	.218
SHERIDAN, PAT	426	1257	166	329	54	9	24	125	51	.376	105	251	.262
SIMMONS, NELSON	84	281	35	73	13	0	10	36	2	.413	28	46	.260
SIMS, DUKE	843	2422	263	580	80	6	100	310	6	.401	338	483	.239
SKIZAS, LOU	239	725	80	196	27	4	30	86	8	.443	50	37	.270
SMALL, JIM	108	141	22	38	6	2	0	10	0	.340	10	22	.270
SMITH, GEORGE	217	634	64	130	27	6	9	57	9	.309	59	142	.205
SMITH, MAYO	73	203	18	43	5	0	0	11	0	.236	36	13	.212
SMITH, WILLIE	691	1654	171	410	63	21	46	211	20	.395	107	284	.248
SOUCHOCK, STEVE	473	1227	163	313	58	20	50	186	15	.457	88	164	.255
SPIKES, CHARLIE	670	2039	240	502	72	12	65	256	27	.389	154	388	.246
SPILMAN, HARRY	401	639	80	151	25	0	16	97	0	.351	61	95	.236
STANLEY, MICKEY	1516	5022	641	1243	201	48	117	500	44	.377	371	564	.248
STAUB, RUSTY	2951	9720	1189	2716	499	47	292	1466	47	.431	1255	888	.279
STEGMAN, DAVE	171	320	39	66	10	2	8	32	5	.325	31	55	.206
SULLIVAN, JOHN	116	259	9	59	5	0	2	18	0	.270	19	45	.228
SUMMERS, CHAMP	698	1371	199	350	63	4	54	218	15	.425	188	244	.255
SUTHERLAND, GARY	1031	3104	308	754	109	10	24	239	11	.308	207	219	.243
SZOTKIEWICZ, KEN	47	84	9	9	1	0	3	9	0	.226	12	29	.107
TAYLOR, BILL	149	173	17	41	8	0	7	26	0	.405	5	39	.237

PLAYER	G	AB	R	H	2B	3B	HR	RBI	SB	SLG	BB	SO	AVG
TAYLOR, TONY	2195	7680	1005	2007	298	86	75	598	234	.352	613	1083	.261
TEBBETTS, BIRDIE	1162	3704	357	1000	169	22	38	469	29	.358	389	261	.270
THOMAS, GEORGE	685	1688	203	430	71	9	46	202	13	.389	138	343	.255
THOMPSON, CHARLIE	187	517	49	123	24	2	8	47	8	.338	39	52	.238
THOMPSON, JASON	1388	4751	634	1243	200	12	208	778	8	.440	798	850	.262
TOLMAN, TIM	107	150	14	26	8	0	5	21	0	.327	1	25	.173
TORGESON, EARL	1668	4969	848	1318	215	46	149	740	133	.417	980	653	.265
TRACEWSKI, DICK	614	1231	148	262	31	9	8	91	15	.272	134	253	.213
TRAMMELL, ALAN	1289	4631	702	1300	214	42	90	504	149	.403	488	519	.281
TRESH, TOM	1192	4251	595	1041	179	34	153	530	45	.411	550	698	.245
TRIANDOS, GUS	1206	3907	389	954	147	6	167	608	1	.413	440	636	.244
TURNER, JERRY	733	1742	222	448	73	9	45	238	45	.272	159	245	.257
TUTTLE, BILL	1270	4268	578	1105	149	47	67	443	38	.363	480	416	.259
VEAL, COOT	247	611	75	141	26	3	1	51	2	.288	56	69	.231
VERYZER, TOM	996	2848	250	687	84	12	14	231	9	.294	143	329	.241
VIRGIL, OSSIE	324	753	75	174	19	7	14	73	6	.331	34	91	.231
WAGNER, MARK	415	842	81	205	20	9	3	71	8	.299	61	130	.243
WALKER, DIXIE	1905	6740	1037	2064	376	96	105	1023	59	.437	817	325	.306
WERTZ, DON	1110	3840	417	929	129	15	77	366	22	.343	389	529	.242
WERTZ, VIC	1862	6099	867	1692	289	42	266	1178	9	.469	828	841	.277
WHITAKER, LOU	1283	4705	724	1320	202	49	93	522	95	.404	576	575	.281
WHITE, JO-JO	877	2652	456	678	83	42	8	229	92	.328	384	276	.256
WILSON, GLENN	676	2358	265	636	130	19	58	316	22	.415	134	394	.270
WISE, CASEY	126	321	37	56	6	3	3	17	2	.240	29	36	.174
WOCKENFUSS, JOHNNY	763	2035	266	537	73	11	86	308	5	.437	269	271	.264
WOOD, JAKE	608	1877	279	469	53	26	35	168	79	.362	159	362	.250
WOODS, RON	582	1247	162	290	34	12	26	130	27	.342	175	171	.233
YORK, RUDY	1603	5891	876	1621	291	52	277	1152	38	.483	791	867	.275
YOST, EDDIE	2109	7346	1215	1863	337	56	139	683	72	.371	1614	920	.254
ZERNIAL, GUS	1234	4131	572	1093	159	22	237	776	15	.486	383	755	.265